To John /
Malcm ith
Good Luck w/ the
Inn.

7/30/08

THE BACK TO BASICS BOOK OF SELLING
A Guide to a Successful Sales Career

ISBN 978-1-4357-2833-2

9 781435 728332

BOOKS BY JOHN R. INGRISANO

The Insurance Dictionary
The Back to Basics Book of Selling
A Perfect Day: Thoughts on Faith & Forgiveness
The Back to Basics Book of Money

The Back to Basics
Book of Selling:
A Guide to a Successful Sales Career

By John R. Ingrisano

Cover Design by April A. Adams
www.AdamsAdmin.com

DEDICATION

For all the people who have supported me over the years with patience, guidance, and ideas, especially two mentors and friends, Dennis E. Hensley, one of the most prolific writers and clear-thinking human beings I've ever met, and Bill Sheridan, who has shared with me his selling, presentation and marketing skills.

I also appreciate and want to thank all the business clients and friends who have placed their trust in me by responding to my sales presentations and paying me, literally, millions of dollars in orders for my products and services over the years.

Finally, to Julie, who inspires me with her steadiness, great smile and integrity.

A NOTE TO READERS

I have always been a salesman, even though I didn't realize it until I was in my 30s. I say that because I love people, I love to talk, and I thoroughly enjoy analyzing problems, coming up with solutions, and "selling" ideas. I enjoy educating people, sharing information, and taking on the challenge of persuading them to see and learn new ideas. In this respect, I see little difference between educators and salespeople.

However, I am not a natural salesman. Some of that terrific breed may exist, but most of the really good salespeople I've seen learned how to communicate and present their ideas through hard work, practice and many mistakes. In fact, one of the best salesmen I ever met (Ben Feldman, who sold more life insurance than anyone in history, and he did it in the blue collar rust-belt city of Youngstown, Ohio) was so shy that he used to do stage presentations from behind a curtain.

My first real job in selling was in life insurance. The agency manager (who must have been desperate to recruit anything that was breathing), told me how great I was going to be, gave me a sales tract and a rate book (this was back before the days of computers), slapped me on the back, and said, "Go get 'em, Tiger!" Like the dog told to go fetch when you pretend to throw the ball, I ran around town for a few days until I realized that I had no idea how to find 'em, how to talk to 'em, or how to sell 'em.

Eventually, through common sense, hard work, reading a lot of books, and getting some good mentoring from people who knew their way around a sales presentation, I began to learn how to sell. Along the way, I also figured out that we all sell, all the time, every day.

My point is that sales skills can be learned. It took me several decades to become respectable at selling, and I keep learning new ideas every day. This book, as the name states, is about the basics. It provides the foundation of how to sell. With every page, you will better understand the art, science and attitude of selling, which means that, with every page, you will get better at what you do.

But knowledge is not enough. Apply what you learn every day. And your sales skills will keep climbing and improving. Good luck and good selling.

    --   John R. Ingrisano
            The Freestyle Entrepreneur
            www.TheFreestyleEntrepreneur.com

ABOUT THE AUTHOR

John R. Ingrisano has been a professional educator and sales trainer since 1975, when he became an instructor of writing and communications at Ball State University. Later, as an insurance consultant, marketing strategist and sales consultant for some of the world's largest financial services, he wrote and produced dozens of sales training and motivational programs, and published thousands of articles and brochures on business, selling skills and the often not-so-fine art of surviving as a small-business owner.

An independent business owner since 1985, he is known as the Voice of the Freestyle Entrepreneur for his roll-up-your-sleeves advice and commentary on his website, www.TheFreestyleEntrepreneur.com, recognized as the place to go for "Survival skills for those of us crazy enough to work for ourselves."

He lives with his company's board of directors (Rocky the Boxer and Toni the Goldie) on the shores of Lake Michigan in Algoma, Wisconsin. He can be reached at john@TheFreestyleEntrepreneur.com.

Foreword

There's an old saying that goes, "Nothing happens until someone sells something." That's not entirely true; things could happen, but not what you want to have happen. Sales and selling are the grease that keeps the economy moving. It's important and there aren't enough people who do it well.

When my partner, Dan Newman, and I bought *Corporate Report Wisconsin* magazine, I was charged with deciding how to improve it. As I reviewed back copies, one thing impressed me: The quality of the columnists. They were a group of talented writers who were capable of bringing our audience of corporate executives, managers and small business owners great information in an interesting manner. It was an easy decision to keep them. We even added another. One of the best is John Ingrisano.

John writes well. He has an innate ability to tell a story. He informs and entertains. His written "voice" is plain and to the point. There is no guessing what he means or where he's coming from and our readers love him. After one of John's recent columns ran, the e-mails poured in. He had written about how he nearly burned himself out – along with several relationships with others – by working too long and hard for a period of time.

His column struck a chord. Spouses wrote in about their experiences and entrepreneurs wrote about how they nearly suffered the same fate as John. Most of all, the readers appreciated his practical, down-to-earth advice on how achieve balance between work and life.

This book on sales is written the same way, in a practical, helpful way that will help you become a better salesperson or turn you into one for the first time. As you begin to enjoy the book, you'll find that John has been selling for some time. Here, he brings you not only the benefit of his selling experience, but those of some very interesting and effective salespeople he's met along the way. As you read, remember that nothing happens until someone sells something, so learn from John – and go make something happen!

Bob Warde
Editorial Director
Corporate Report Wisconsin magazine

TABLE OF CONTENTS

Chapter One

Products Do Not
Sell Themselves

It was once widely believed that, "If a man can ... make a better mousetrap than his neighbor, though he builds his house in the woods the world will make a beaten path to his door." That quote is attributed to Ralph Waldo Emerson. And while Emerson was one of America's finest essayists, philosophers, and poets, he certainly was no businessman. No product, no matter how good it may be, will sell itself. It has to be sold. And that is a fact of life.

Almost daily, the business section of any newspaper tells us about new companies – many with innovative ideas and surefire products -- that have gone belly up. The "Public Notice" and "Auction" columns in classified sections tell the same story: Companies have declared bankruptcy and what is left of their capital assets has to be auctioned off to pay their debts. Many of these companies do not fail because of high overhead, inefficiency, or managerial incompetence. All too often, they fail because the founders invested all their time and money in developing that better mousetrap, with no effort given to developing a marketing strategy. They failed to realize that customers were not going to beat down their doors to shove money across the counter for their products.

Products have to be marketed. Products have to be sold. An obscure footnote to history tells us that, were it not for a salesman named Vail, Alexander Graham Bell's venture with the telephone might never have gotten off the ground. H.J. Heinz, the founder of the company that bears his name, did not develop those "57 Varieties" by sitting and waiting for customers to come to him. When he first started in business, he loaded his products into a wheelbarrow every day and sold them door to door. Mr.

Wrigley and his chewing gum became famous because he "hit the streets," so to speak, and sold his product from a basket.

That famous Texan named Mary Kay Ash is another great example. Starting in 1963, she built a storefront cosmetics business into Mary Kay Cosmetics, a nationally known, multibillion-dollar empire that continues to grow by leaps and bounds. How did she build this empire? Is it because her products are better than the hundreds of others that enter the market and fail each year? Mary Kay cosmetics are good products, but quality of product alone does not explain this incredible success. What made the company successful was marketing. Selling. Mary Kay Cosmetics continues to boast a sales network that is second to none, and in 2006 racked up wholesale sales of $2.25 billion.

Remember, it is not the quality of a product alone that determines its failure or success. Products do not sell themselves. They need to be sold. If you were to examine two companies, each with equally competent management, which offered identical products, you would see that the company that understands the importance of marketing the product, of selling the product, of bringing the public into contact with the product, this will be the more successful of the two.

Products can be sold by any of a thousand techniques — advertising, promotional campaigns, free samples, etc. Small nickel-and-dime items can be sold without the aid of a salesperson. Cigarettes, gum, soft drinks, and similar items can be bought from a machine, buyer awareness having been piqued through media advertising and attractive displays. Many such purchases are impulse buys, which satisfy basic needs or simple whim. While a "media blitz" or eye-catching merchandising may soften up buyer resistance, most major products or services require one-on-one contact between a prospective buyer and a sales professional if they are going to sell at all, much less realize their maximum level of sales. Good advertising can attract prospective buyers, but it takes a sales professional to turn the curious into customers.

The Role of the Sales Professional

The sales professional plays a unique role in society and in our economy. He or she is a facilitator, a catalyst —- someone who makes things happen. It was a sales professional who convinced Grandpa to replace his push mower with one of the revolutionary self-propelled models. It was a sales professional who sold you the latest top-of-the-line techno gizmo with all the options you hadn't realized were available. The sales professional is the link between the manufacturer and the buyer, between an innovative service and the people who "discover" its many features and benefits.

It takes a sales professional -- a person skilled in identifying needs of prospective buyers, making the buyers aware of those needs, and identifying the product or course of action which will meet those needs -- to communicate to prospects *how* a product will meet their needs and *why* they should buy it ... and buy it (A) now and (B) from you.

In retail business, the prospective buyer comes to the salesperson. But just because an individual walks in the door does not mean that he is going to buy. He may just be window shopping, may not immediately see what he wants, or may have a number of questions that he wants answered before he makes a decision.

How many times have you walked into a store, especially during the holiday season, with a desire to buy "something" extravagant for your spouse or children? You may be out of your area of expertise (a husband in search of a coat for his wife or a wife looking for a new power tool for her husband's workbench) and desperately in need of sales assistance. But either no one shows up with an offer to help, or the one who does is indifferent or unknowledgeable and of no value at all. You probably end up making a blind stab at buying something that you pray turns out to be right, or you make tracks to the door. The store lost a sale, or made a smaller sale than it could have, because the all-important ingredient -- an interested, motivated, knowledgeable professional salesperson --- was lacking.

Now look at the other side of the coin. Think of the stores you have entered where you were greeted by a courteous, interested salesperson, a person who knew his or her products and made the extra effort to provide you with exactly what you needed. Such a person probably also knew how to maximize a sale:

"We have a lovely blouse that will go very nicely with that skirt. Let me show you."

"This car features a top quality six-stack CD player and all-around airbags as standard equipment, and is one of the top-rated models for mileage. And did you know that this is our most popular seller."

"What would you like to drink with your order? Can I interest you in some apple pie today?"

Think about how questions such as these maximize sales. In the first example, a woman has entered a store with the intention of buying a skirt. She is not opposed to buying anything else; she simply hasn't given it any thought. But she knows that she wants to buy the skirt. The salesperson makes the simple suggestion that she might also want to look at a blouse. The suggestion is courteous and helpful, certainly not high pressure. The customer would only have to say, "No, thank you, this will be fine," to decline. There is no risk, no loss, no penalty to the salesperson — but there is a very good chance of making that additional sale.

Suppose that each week the store sells 100 skirts for $50 each, grossing $5,000. The salesperson earns a 10% commission on every sale, so she earns

$500 a week. Now suppose that every time a customer buys a skirt, the salesperson recommends a blouse priced at $30 to go with it. If only a quarter of those customers buy a blouse, the store will gross an additional *$750*, and the salesperson will earn an additional *$75*. Both the store and the salesperson would realize a 15% increase in income, all because of a simple suggestion. In addition, because of the professional, courteous sales attention, customers will probably come back again, becoming regular clients of the store.

The same concept applies to business, industrial, and financial services sales. After closing a major order, the office machine salesperson might suggest, "We have a special attachment for this machine which would allow you to use it in your accounting area as well. It will double your capacity at only a fraction of the cost." After completing an application for life insurance on a husband, the life agent might ask, "How's Mary's coverage? With both of you working, there'd be quite a financial loss if anything happened to her."

The sales professional makes the difference when it comes to both *making the sale and maximizing the sale.* This is perhaps best illustrated in an anecdote told by an associate years ago. When asked, "What's a salesperson?" he replied:

> *"Let me tell you what a salesperson is. A fellow walked into a department store and asked for a sales job. Since the applicant had no previous sales experience, the manager was naturally leery. But having a soft heart, he said, 'I'll give you one day to prove yourself. You can start right away in sporting goods.'*
>
> *Later in the day, the sales manager dropped by to see how his new salesman was doing and found him talking to a customer. 'You've made a good selection. This is a terrific fishing rod, the best we carry. But you know, the really big fish aren't by the shore. You have to get out into the middle of the lake. What you need is a boat.' The customer hesitated for a moment, but finally agreed. The salesman*

went on. 'Of course, by the time you row out to where the really big fish are biting, you'll be too exhausted to enjoy yourself. Fortunately, we have a motor that's just right for that boat. And you won't find it for a better price anywhere in town.' The customer couldn't turn down a deal like that, so he bought the motor, too. 'Now, that should just about do it,' the salesman concluded, and then hesitated. 'How are you going to get that boat to the lake?" he asked. The customer didn't know, and it wasn't long before the new salesman had sold him a trailer.

When the customer left, the sales manager came rushing over. 'You're terrific! You just made the single biggest sale in the history of our store! And just think, all because the customer came in to buy a fishing pole.' The new salesman looked at the sales manager and said, 'He didn't come in to buy a fishing pole. He wandered in, and we started chatting. When he mentioned that his wife was in the next department buying shoes because she was going to her sister's for the weekend, I told him it sounded like a dull couple of days for him and asked if he'd ever thought of taking up fishing.' Now that's a salesman!"

What Is Selling?

Does selling make a difference? Without a doubt. But what is selling? If you asked 100 sales professionals to write down their definitions of selling, you would probably get 103 different answers. Selling is a science. It is an art. It is a system. It is an active, step-by-step process of guidance and motivation, involving a logical sequence of planned events. And it is more. But in its simplest form, just about everyone could agree with the following definition:

SELLING IS THE ACTIVE PROCESS OF PRESENTING INFORMATION IN SUCH A MANNER THAT IT MOTIVATES AND GUIDES THE OTHER PARTY TO TAKE A SPECIFIC ACTION.

Making a sale is very much like opening a combination lock or dialing the correct sequence of numbers to place a telephone call. Most of all, selling is what *you* do. It is not just a considerate service or a luxury. It is a vital link in the business chain. Without exception, selling makes the difference between a good year and a bad one, between a company's success and its failure, and, in many ways, between prosperity and sluggishness in our economy. If you doubt this, keep in mind that there was money during the Great Depression; it didn't suddenly disappear. But it didn't move or circulate. It didn't go anywhere. The people who had money were not spending it. Instead, they were literally stuffing it into their mattresses.

The Great Depression was caused by a number of complex factors, and I am not suggesting that platoons of super-motivated, super-qualified professionals could have single-handedly stimulated the economy. What I am saying is that if every salesperson in the country stayed home for a month and did not attempt to sell, sales would plummet and our whole economy would stagger. People would continue to buy their daily necessities and might even seek out other items. But across the nation, sales would shrivel by as much as 10% -- even 20% or 30%. And we would be on the road to another depression.

Selling counts. Selling keeps the wheels of the economy turning. That is because, with rare exception, products do not sell themselves. They have to be sold. And they need to be sold by motivated, interested sales professionals.

Why a Book on the Basics?

The sales process is really fairly simple. It's a lot like riding a bicycle — once you have it mastered, it becomes second nature. But for the person who has never gotten on a bike before, God's creation of the universe wouldn't appear to be much more difficult. Selling, like riding a bike, is essentially a matter of mastery.

But hold on, all you six-figure sales pros out there: Before you begin writing letters in protest, let's clarify one point: No one ever said that selling is easy. And I'm not saying it, either. In fact, it takes a lot of hard work to be successful in sales. And once salesmanship is mastered, it can always be improved. Like any profession, selling requires continuous education, growth, and development.

The basics, however, are simple to learn ... even they may take a lifetime to master. And these basics are the foundation upon which everything else is built. When you have a firm grasp of the basics, doors of opportunity and success are flung open ... wide open. But without the basics, you will go nowhere, no matter how hard you work.

Over the years a number of "Secrets to Success" and "Shortcuts to Success" in selling have been developed. There really are no secrets, no shortcuts. A working understanding of psychology, for instance, may help you fine tune your sales skills. Tracking your biorhythms may give you added confidence and help you be at your best. Learning how to read the prospect's eye movement or body language can't hurt. But these are add--ons, extras to help you refine the fundamental approaches to selling. It is crucial that you first learn to walk with these fundamentals. Then, and only then, can you run with the extras.

Why is a mastery of the basics so important? Because the basic principles of selling never really change. The fundamentals of effective salesmanship are still essentially the same as they were when the serpent sold Eve on the benefits of that apple. They are founded on the concepts of an understanding of human nature and a whole lot of common sense. The basic principles of selling have been tested, refined, and improved through years of use — not only by tens of thousands of successful salespeople, but also by politicians, writers, and business people who have shaped the history of the world.

Think of selling as effective, persuasive communication, because that is exactly what it is. The ancient Greeks developed oratory, known today as public speaking. The Romans raised it to an art form. The citizen who could persuade his audience, convincing them of the truth of an idea or the value of a particular course of action, was honored with laurels, riches, and prestige.

Such persuasive oration was recreated by William Shakespeare in his play *The Tragedy of Julius Caesar*. Marc Antony's address at Caesar's funeral begins, "Friends, Romans, countrymen, lend me your ears! I come to bury Caesar, not to praise him. The evil that men do lives after them, the good is oft interred with their bones; so let it be with Caesar." Marc Antony goes on to convince the crowd that there was good in Caesar and that they should rise up against his murderers. Another example of effective oratory is the political tract, *Common Sense*. Written by the pro-American English essayist and revolutionary, Thomas Paine, *Common Sense* argues forcefully and persuasively for the freedom of the American colonies.

Every time a politician opens his mouth, he is selling something. Every time a writer uncaps her pen, she is selling something. Every time a 16-year-old boy asks a girl out for a date, he is selling something. And to present their ideas effectively, they use various tools of persuasion that have been developed and refined over the centuries. The words may be different, the ideas may be different — but the techniques they use do not change.

Writers, politicians, and orators sell ideas. You sell your product, whether it's life insurance, automobiles, office machinery, toothpaste, a training program, accounting or therapeutic massage service. But no matter *what* you sell, the fundamentals of *how* you sell will be the same. The techniques have not changed for centuries. They will work for you just as they did for

Socrates, Aristotle, William Shakespeare, Thomas Paine, and others.

The bottom line: Since the basic, time-tested techniques of selling work, since they do the job, there is no need for you to re-invent the wheel. You do not have to start from scratch, learning how to become a successful sales professional through trial and error. You can learn from the experiences of others. As the saying goes, "If it ain't broke, don't fix it." And the basic techniques of successful sound selling "ain't broke." Every day they are used effectively by tens of thousands of individuals in tens of thousands of situations.

Four Ingredients

You don't need to be a genius or have a Ph.D. in marketing to be a successful sales professional. All you need are four things:

1. A thorough knowledge of your product or service.

2. A firm commitment to work hard and to invest the time and effort it will take to become successful. Andrew Carnegie, one of the most successful industrialists ever born, had the philosophy that, "Anything worth having is worth working for."

3. A winning attitude.

4. A mastery of the basic, fundamental techniques of successful selling.

This book can't tell you anything about your product. You must take the time to become as familiar with it as possible. This book cannot tell you how hard you should work (although I will make a few suggestions). Some people think that an eight-hour workday represents four hours of over-time, while others regularly work up to 16 hours a day. And while we can tell you how to develop a winning attitude, we cannot instill one in you. What this book will do is equip you with a firm understanding of the key elements involved in the process of successful selling.

As should be clear by now, the ideas in this book are not new. They're not revolutionary and they're not fancy. They are simply a compilation of the basic concepts of the techniques, which have proven over the years to be successful for countless numbers of sales professionals and others. These ideas should be thoroughly learned, step by step. Most of all, they should be *understood*. Do not look at this book as sales training. Look at it as sales education! If you understand the purpose of each step in the successful sales process, you will be able to apply it with more conviction than if you simply view it as a step to be blindly followed, because the guy who wrote the book told you to.

Study the basics. Master them. Perfect them. Once you have a solid understanding of all of the elements of successful selling and can see how they all fit together, you can begin fine tuning and adjusting them to fit your own sales situation and sales style. Make them yours. In turn, they will make you an effective, successful sales professional.

Chapter Two

Selling as a Profession

Some folks actually believe that selling is rather like the old misconception about teaching: people go into it because they are not capable of doing anything else. Wrong on both counts. Still, some people actually believe it. What's worse, a number of salespeople — who should know better — believe it too. They look at selling as a job that has been forced upon them by circumstances. They act as if they are ashamed to call on other people to talk about their products or services. They mumble something about being "sales associates," "product representatives," or "consulting advisors" when asked what they do for a living.

They do not trust their products, they do not believe in their profession, they do not have faith in themselves. And it shows. To them, selling is nothing more than a job, a job of which they are not very proud and, as a result, a job at which they are not very good.

But selling is — and should be perceived as — a profession, an honorable, respectable profession. A profession is a career to which the individual devotes his or her entire life. The professional never stops learning, never stops growing, never stops striving to improve skills and talents. Professionals are not just doctors or lawyers. In fact, there are many doctors and lawyers around who are far from being professionals. On the other hand, there are a number of salespeople who are sterling examples of the word "professionalism." A degree does not make someone a professional. Professionalism is the result of an attitude, a state of mind, a sense of pride in what you do, and a determination to do it well.

If you have doubts whether selling is going to be your profession or just a job, you should reevaluate your own attitude toward your work. Because selling will be whatever you make it: just a job, or a professional career.

As for the misguided impressions a vocal minority harbors about salespeople, the best defense is a thick skin toward their ignorance and a lot of patience. You have probably encountered some of these people already: those people who, when they heard about your decision to enter sales, reacted as if you were carrying a highly contagious social disease. They turn cool, quickly withdraw their hand, and make it quite clear that, whatever it is you sell, they are quite sure they already have enough. They may even express sympathy because you were unable to get a "real" job. They do not know or care that your decision to enter sales was a positive one, motivated by the opportunity to earn a good income while providing a valuable service.

Fortunately, though vocal, these people are few. They speak from a position of ignorance. They see salespeople as a stereotype: glad-handing, slightly shifty, gaudily dressed hawkers of overpriced merchandise, like the Herb Tarlick of the 1970s TV show, *WKRP*. But forget about these stereotypes. Yes, there are huckster salespeople, just as there are dishonest doctors and profane ministers. But on the whole, most people are honest and hardworking. Those who enjoy hanging negative stereotype labels on others are not worth fighting. Why? For one thing, you are not going to be able to fight this prejudice, primarily because the vocal minority who hold such views enjoy their ignorance. Trying to change their way of thinking would be like trying to persuade a man to come down off a compost pile when the fact of the matter is that he rather enjoys sitting there. Besides, you have better things to do than worry about the opinions of the vocal minority. But for both your own sanity and for the information of anyone else, be aware of a few facts about the profession of selling and the dedicated individuals known as sales professionals.

1. EVERYONE SELLS SOMETHING

The young man asking a girl for a date. The lawyer pleading her case before the judge. The executive attempting to sway the opinion of the company's board of directors toward a new product line or marketing strategy. The husband explaining to his wife how a new sports car really is a good buy, even if it will not hold all six of their kids. Look around. Examples are everywhere. People are constantly trying to motivate, convince and persuade others to see a certain point of view or take a specified action. Everyone sells something, be it an image, an idea, or a tangible product. Politicians sell their integrity, honesty and suitability to be elected. Doctors not only sell their services, but also their "bedside manner" when dealing with patients. All of us, in both our personal and business relationships, want the other person to view us or something we have to offer in a certain way.

Look at how we handle our relationships with others. In the broadest sense, we all want to be liked. We all want to be thought of as likable, as nice. We all want to be accepted. As a result, we all spend a great deal of time trying to look, sound or behave in a manner which "sells" us to our friends, business associates, customers, and acquaintances. If you have any doubts, look at the clothes you are wearing right now. Though you may not be a slave to fads, your clothes are probably reasonably in fashion. Why? Because it is the norm. It is what is accepted and expected.

Think back to when you were a teenager. Every boy either slicked up or dressed down (depending upon the decade) to impress a young woman who either dressed up or pulled on wrinkled jeans for the same purpose. And today? Though the three-piece business suit is no longer the uniform of office cadres, we do wear the latest "business casual" or "office dress" when at work around others. (And, yes, if you sell pharmaceuticals to farmers, you may show up in a sports coat or pants suit, but you also have a pair of mud-kickers in the trunk, all of which is part of the "dress code" for your market.) Do not we all like to project or sell an image that we are a little better off financially than we really are? That we are a little brighter?

A little more hardworking? A little nicer? And that's fine. That's human nature. Just as long as we remember that everyone sells something. Because, as we pointed out in Chapter One:

> **SELLING IS THE ACTIVE PROCESS**
> **OF PRESENTING INFORMATION**
> **IN SUCH A MANNER THAT**
> **IT MOTIVATES AND GUIDES**
> **THE OTHER PARTY**
> **TO TAKE A SPECIFIED ACTION.**

What is that specified action? In the case of the teenager, it is the implicit (and sometimes explicit) approval of peers and members of the opposite sex. In the case of the doctor, it is recognition as a dedicated, responsible physician. For the executive, it is the approval of and reward by superiors. For the sales professional, it is the acceptance and purchase of a product or service by a customer or client. And all this leads to the second truth about selling:

2. SELLING IS AN HONORABLE PROFESSION

It has been said that selling makes and keeps the wheels of an economy turning smoothly. The fact is that, without selling, the wheels of the economy would not turn at all. If they existed at all, they would quickly fall off. As we said earlier, selling is a productive activity in that it brings about an efficient exchange of goods and services. It results in lower prices and greater production.

The sales professional earns his or her keep. He or she provides a valuable service that directly benefits people. As a businessperson, he or she does not sit back in a make-work position and shuffle papers to earn a salary. The sales professional earns by doing. The sales professional earns by selling.

The Benefits of a Career in Sales

Not only is a career in sales a valuable and prestigious profession, but it also offers a number of opportunities not to be found in any other field. These include:

- *Unlimited income potential.* Most people either punch a time clock or earn a fixed salary. For the majority, statistics tell us that the median annual household income in this country is about $50,000. That averages out to $25,000 a year for two-income families, or just over $500 a week.

  You read of labor negotiations in which the new contract calls for a five percent or seven percent an hour increase, phased in over several years. A five percent increase means a raise of $25 a week, or $300 a year. Not only is the increase rather paltry, but, the real frustrating part is that the individual's earnings are dictated not so much by his or her own efforts and initiative, but by the going rate for that job at that time.

  On the other hand, as a commission-earning sales professional, your income is limited only by your willingness to work, to learn, and to sell. No one sets your salary or gives you a raise . . . except you. As a result, your income potential is virtually unlimited. Do you want to make $50,000 a year? How about $80,000 a year? Or $100,000? $150,000? Or even $500,000? It is possible. It may not be easy, but it is possible. And you can sit down today, based on your commission schedule, and calculate *exactly* how much you have to sell of your product to earn that kind of money.

  If you doubt that it is possible, look at the example of Ben Feldman, often touted the greatest life insurance agent who has ever lived. He started out with a goal of selling $1 million of life insurance in a year. He made that goal. So he set his next goal at $2 million in a single year, double his previous record. He made that, too. Then he set his goal at $1 million of sales in a single month, or $12 million of sales a year! Once he made that, he went for $1 million per *week* . . . and he accomplished that goal, as well. His earnings? They increased dramatically also. And he was able to do it because he is in sales, because he set his goals and, through his own determination, hard work and perseverance, he made it happen. You can make it happen, too.

Want a $300 a raise? Well, if you are paid 10% commission on every sale, and your average sale is $1,000, that means that by making just three more sales, you have just give yourself a raise of $300. Want a bigger raise. Keep selling. The choice is yours.

- *Freedom to be your own boss.* You may have a sales manager or marketing director whose job is to be sure you are on track with your sales goals. However, as a rule, you are on your own. No one will be looking over your shoulder, handing you assignments, or making sure you get to work on time. Your commission check may come from the company whose products you sell, and your sales manager may want to keep track of your sales activity. But you really have only one boss: *yourself.*

You are the decision maker in your career. You are responsible for setting your own working hours, keeping your own appointments, selecting your own prospects and tracking your own performance. In most instances, you have the best of both worlds. You have the support and backing of the company for which you work. But you also work for yourself. You could not ask for a sweeter arrangement.

Paying the Piper

If selling is the greatest thing since the discovery that people come in two sexes, why isn't everyone in sales? And why aren't they all millionaires? The answer is simple. Selling is hard, hard work. But as many gave discovered, selling is the best-paid hard work there is!

While selling does offer the greatest rewards of any profession, there is a price the successful sales professional must be willing to pay. Becoming a successful sales professional requires a great deal of:

- *Hard work.* Good old-fashioned perspiration is one of the most important ingredients in a sales career. You must be willing, especially early in your career, to put in long hours learning the business, improving and polishing your sales skills, and establishing a solid customer base. Few sales professionals who are successful today started out by working the bare minimum of 40 hours per week. Many worked as many as 60, 70, and even 80 hours a week the first several years.

  Selling pays off. In no other profession is it truer than in sales that you get out of it exactly what you put in — nothing more, nothing less. Yes, you may find it necessary to devote long hours that might be considered excessive by some other standards. However, that kind of devotion pays off. If you are willing to pay *your* dues and put in the amount of hard work required to make a success of it, selling can truly be for you "the best paid hard work there is."

- *Self-discipline.* As you have probably surmised by now, selling is not for the individual who wants to work only when the urge strikes. To put in the calls necessary, to put in the hours necessary, to do the job right, requires a great deal of self-discipline.

  A few pages back you learned that one of the benefits of selling is being your own boss. That is the good news. The bad news is that, as your own boss, you have to work for one of the meanest, toughest, most unsympathetic slave drivers you have ever encountered. You must resist the temptation to take off and catch a ball game on a sunny summer day or sleep in because you stayed up too late the night before. Though your sales manager may help, you are the one who has to set your own objectives, develop a plan for meeting those objectives, and then stick to that plan, day in and day out, rain or shine, to make those objectives become reality. You must be tougher on yourself than any other boss could ever be.

- *Self-motivation.* The late Johnny Carson had been on TV for decades. There were certainly times when he did not feel well, was tired, had personal problems on his mind, or was just not in the mood to entertain those millions of "Tonight Show" viewers. But he did. Night after night he went on stage and attempted to give the best performance of his life, presenting an amusing, entertaining monologue and hosting a bevy of America's celebrities with enthusiasm, charm and wit.

How did he do it? He had learned the art of self-motivation. He did not merely hope to be in the right mood, to have a charged-up, positive attitude for each show. He knew that he *must* be ready to give his best each and every night. His continued success depended on it. And, let's face it, he could not possibly always have been in that right mood. There were times when he had to consciously put himself in that mood, put himself in the right frame of mind. He had to motivate himself to maintain a positive attitude.

Johnny Carson never let his mood dictate to him how he would feel and what he would do. He used his mind to dictate and control what his mood would be. He was always in control of his attitude, not at its mercy.

As a professional salesperson, you must be able to do the same thing. You must learn to develop and maintain within yourself a positive, motivated attitude. Regardless of your mood, you must be "on stage." Because attitude counts as a key element in successful selling, both from the point of how it affects you and, in turn, how it affects your prospective buyers. In fact, attitude and self-motivation rank right up there with sheer hard work as the most important characteristics a sales professional can possess.

Why is it so important to be able to motivate yourself and maintain a positive mental attitude? It is important because selling is based on the law of averages. Not even the greatest salesperson in the world bats a thousand. You may spend hours on the phone calling prospective customers before you find one who has the time and the interest to talk to you. You may drive miles to an appointment, only to find that the person you were scheduled to meet "left the office ten minutes ago."

When you make a sale, you will be on top of the world, convinced that you can do no wrong. But there will be times when you begin to think no one in the entire world wants to see you or hear about your or your products. You'll become tired; you'll get depressed. There will be times when, in spite of what you know in your head, in your heart you will feel you'll never get another appointment or make another sale for as long as you live. And that kind of thinking can be deadly. In fact, more promising sales careers end in failure because of a deteriorating attitude than for any other reason. They do not end for lack of ability. They do not end because of laziness or even because of ignorance about proper sales techniques. Most promising sales careers fail because of a destructive, negative attitude.

A bad attitude is deadly because it does not affect only the salesperson. It also can be sensed by the prospect. When a salesperson gets on the phone or goes into the interview thinking he or she is likely to fail, that lack of confidence comes through as if it were being broadcast on a public address system. Take the young man who calls up a girl for a date, convinced she will turn him down. Believing the battle is lost before a shot is fired, he calls up ready, willing, almost eager to accept defeat. And he gets it. When she answers the phone, he whines: "Hello, Sally, you wouldn't want to go out with me, would you?" He is almost begging her to say "no," and chances are she will. On the other hand, what if the young man starts off with a confident tone in his voice and says something like, "Hello, Sally, that new Johnny Depp movie is in town, and unless you have plans Friday night, I'd like you to join me. Can I pick you up around 7:30?" Just by being more positive, he will double or triple his odds of getting that date.

Why is self-motivation so important? Because it can make the difference between success and failure. Because when all else fails, the ability to get yourself charged up and keep yourself going can and will bring you through a number of rough spots. When things start looking gloomy, you need to be able to "kick start" yourself back into a positive frame of mind.

What if you are not by nature a glowing optimist? How do you develop this crucial ability? There is no simple answer. In Chapter Ten, we will deal with this subject in detail, but for the moment, simply remember that it is possible to change your outlook, to imbue yourself with a positive mental attitude and the ability to motivate yourself, and that many a glowing optimistic success today was once a depressed, negative loser.

- *An interest in people.* Selling is a people business. If you would rather lock yourself up in an office of if you tend to shy away from social contact, selling is probably not for you.

But if you get a kick out of people, like meeting new folks, making new friends, then you are in the right business. The successful sales professional must have a genuine interest in people, enjoy working with them, and care about them. That is something that cannot be faked. Nothing will cool a customer's interest faster than insincerity, no matter how well disguised you may think it is. The successful sales professional sees customers as more than just a commission check. He or she genuinely cares about the customer's needs and becomes successful by meeting those needs.

- *A dab of horse sense.* Not only must you like people if you are to be successful in sales, you must also learn what motivates them and what makes them tick, especially in the sales situation. There are many different types of people, each with their own likes, dislikes, attitudes and opinions. While one individual may purchase your product because of your charming personality and sweet disposition, another may not care if you are the rudest person in the world, as long as you can provide the right product for the right price, and follow up with continuing service.

You must train yourself to interpret and analyze "where each prospect is coming from" and react accordingly to the needs and style of each individual. For instance, some people need to feel that they are in control at all times. They resent anyone who they suspect is trying to make a decision for them. Others want someone to do just that — lead them by the hand and make their decision for them. Then there are people who do not want to hear all the technical hocus-pocus. Just tell them what your product will do, what the benefits of owning it will be. The flip side of the coin is the prospect who wants to hear nothing but the raw facts and figures.

There is a great deal that can be said on this subject of the psychology of selling. Many studies have been conducted on the "mind" of the buyer. The results could — and do — fill shelf after shelf of libraries. The type of person who buys what, why, and from whom has been analyzed and classified in dozens of ways. You could make a lifetime study of the psychological makeup of the buying public. But you could also do just as well with a little good old-fashioned horse sense. Simply learn to listen to prospects. Learn to observe their moods, their attitudes, their distractions.

An example of the effective use of common sense and the powers of observation can be seen in the story about a salesman who showed up for a scheduled appointment with an executive. Just as he was about to begin his presentation, the phone rang. It was the executive's wife, calling from the hospital, with news that their son had fallen and broken his arm. It was a clean break, everything was under control, and the wife reassured the executive that there was no need for him to come to the hospital. She just wanted him to be aware of what had happened and let him know that they might not be back by the time he got home from work. The executive hung up the phone and, trying to follow his wife's advice not to worry, asked the salesman to continue with his presentation.

The salesman, possessing a healthy amount of good common sense, did not even attempt to continue. He knew that the executive, no matter how cool and calm he appeared to be on the outside, and in spite of his wife's reassurances, had only one thing on his mind: his son. Instead of attempting to continue with a presentation that would only be half heard, he suggested they reschedule the interview for some time next week. But he did not let it go at that. Instead of just leaving, he suggested to his prospect that he might want to go see his son. And since the executive had commuted by train to work that day and did not have a car at his disposal, the salesman went the extra mile and drove the executive to the hospital himself. You can be darned sure that the presentation he postponed that day became a sale the next time they met.

Just remember that each prospect is different and each sales situation is different. The successful sales professional must be able to understand both the way people tend to behave in most situations and at the same time be able to play it by ear when the need arises.

- *Organization.* Anybody can make a sale, given enough time, enough prospects, and enough perseverance. But the successful sales professional does more than make a sale now and then. He or she sells for a living and sells consistently, every day, every week, every month, every year. For that reason, and in order to maintain that consistency in sales, the successful salesperson, the individual who is committed to a long-term career in sales, must be organized.

Being organized requires planning, training, scheduling your time, and preparing for each interview. This book will show you how to do just that. In fact, that is what this book is all about: the process of selling, with all that makes it effective. Because selling is not a haphazard, hit-or-miss, random activity. It is a well-organized, highly polished process.

Monsters in the Sales Professional's Mind

We all have fears, second thoughts, doubts. If we say we do not, we are either fools or liars. These fears are like the monster that lived in the basement when we were kids. We may have never seen it, but we think we heard it from time to time. And the longer it lived down there, the bigger it got. There are usually some monsters in every new salesperson's mind. The sooner you realize that these fears are normal, understandable, and can easily be dealt with, the sooner you can get on with the positive job of building your career. Let's examine some of those fears and doubts, hold them up to the light and see if we can dispatch them.

1. *Fear of the unknown*, which is a perfectly logical fear. Every day you are meeting new people, walking into situations you have never encountered before. There is nothing safe about selling. Every day you cover new ground. Many new salespersons teeter on the brink of panic at the thought of knocking on another office door or dialing one more number for an appointment. Occasionally, an adventuresome soul comes along who enjoys charging boldly into new situations. Most of us, however, are usually a bit apprehensive about unfamiliar surroundings and circumstances. It is normal. It is natural.

2. *Fear of failure*. This actually encompasses two fears. The first deals directly with income. You may have left a position with a secure weekly or monthly salary. Every month, come rain or shine, that check was placed in your hand or deposited into your account. All of a sudden, that is no longer the case. As a commission-earning sales professional, you are paid for what you sell, and only when you sell it. Suddenly you think, "What if I don't sell anything?" or "What if I don't sell enough?" This fear is also normal. However, if you learn and apply the principles of successful selling, you will sell, you will earn, you will succeed. Adjust your thinking to the changed manner in which you now earn your income. Track your expenses. Budget your dollars. Most of all, relax and be confident. Remember, while you may work harder — perhaps for a while and earn less than you did before — eventually your income should far outstrip anything you had earned previously. Though there are no blind guarantees, the odds are in your favor, provided you are willing to work hard.

The second aspect of fear of failure stems from fear of failing as a sales professional. What happens if you spend an hour with a prospective buyer, make the best presentation of your life, and at the end the prospect simply yawns and says, "Thanks, but I'm not interested"? The error is in assuming that because you failed to make a particular sale, that you yourself are a failure. There is no connection between the two. In fact, salespeople do not fail because they lose one sale, or two, or three, or even a hundred. They fail because they stop *trying* to make sales. Remember that no one ever succeeded without running the risk of failure. And the greater the risk, the greater the possible degree of success. Anyone who knows baseball knows that Babe Ruth was a home run king. What many people do not realize, however, is that he was also a strikeout king. He consistently struck out more than anybody else. But quite literally he never stopped trying. Neither should you. Do not count the times you strike out. Track the home runs, the successful sales.

3. *Fear of rejection.* As we mentioned earlier, everyone wants to be liked, everyone likes to be wanted. And the problem some new salespeople have is that they take business rejections personally. They equate rejection of an idea or of their product with rejection of themselves. To become a successful sales professional, you will have to accept the fact that there are going to be times when a door is slammed in your face or someone hangs up on you. But most of the time, unless you are an obnoxious, irresponsible buffoon, what is being rejected is your product, not you. Or perhaps prospects are resisting what they perceive to be an invasion of their privacy, the result of their own self-imposed mental barrier. In Chapter Six, we will discuss some of the things that typically go through a prospect's mind during the interview. For now, just remember that while some people will say "no" because you may not have clearly presented your product or they simply do not want to purchase it, this rarely has anything to do with you as a person. And although it is sometimes difficult to separate rejection of product from rejection of you, that is exactly what you have to do.

4. *Fear of prospects.* Some sales professionals feel awkward when cast as

the seller in the buyer-seller relationship. They have this nagging apprehension that the prospect will not pay attention, will not take them seriously or, worse, will become hostile. However, the fact of the matter is that few of these fears ever come true. They rank on the probability chart with fear of being hit by a meteor.

Call Reluctance: The Dread Disease

These are some of the typical fears or concerns that go through the minds of most salespersons at some time, usually at the start of their careers. Some people experience all of them; some just one or two. Some people become stricken with terror; others get a mild case of butterflies in the stomach. But no matter what the fear — and no matter what the degree — these fears manifest almost inevitably in the form of a deadly disease known as *call reluctance.*

Call reluctance is what makes grown men and women pull the covers over their heads and decide to sleep in because it is raining outside. It makes some salespeople drive around the prospect's block for an hour, stand on the doorstep for another hour, and then decide that it is too late to call, so they might as well go home. Call reluctance is what can make cowards of the best salespeople — if they let it get out of control.

Call reluctance is just what its name implies: a reluctance, a hesitation to put oneself in front of prospective buyers. And it may be for any or all of the reasons we mentioned earlier. It may be fear of the unknown; fear of failure; fear of rejection; fear of prospects . . . or just plain fear!

Call reluctance can be deadly. It can drain your energy, ruin your health, and destroy a promising sales career. It will keep you from doing the one thing you must do to become and remain a success in sales: talk to prospective buyers. Most of all, it can destroy an optimistic, charged-up attitude and instill fear, lack of confidence, and unhappiness.

Because call reluctance is so deadly, it is important to identify it and nip it in the bud before it gets a hold on you. Call reluctance materializes in several ways. One dead giveaway is the problem of paperwork. True, there is always a certain amount of paperwork involved in being a sales professional. But it should never be allowed to cut into your prime selling time. Letting it get out of hand is like letting the tail wag the dog. The more time you spend catching up on your correspondence, the less time you spend out in the field making sales. If you find yourself skipping appointments because you simply have to finish your Christmas card list, something is wrong — and needs to be corrected quickly.

A second symptom of call reluctance is procrastination. Examples include waiting for two weeks to call on a really hot prospect; or preparing all morning to get on the phone and set up appointments — sharpening pencils, looking up phone numbers, straightening your tie, combing your hair, getting another cup of coffee — and then knocking off for lunch without having made a single call.

Another symptom of call reluctance has been dubbed the "bad weather blues." This is sort of a catchall symptom. You cannot make calls because it is too hot, too cold, raining, snowing, or possibly too sunny. The weather is not right. The time is too late. There is always something. The reasons all may sound good at the moment. But the bottom line is that, when all is said and done, nothing has been done.

Another example of call reluctance is psychosomatic illness. Kids get it on a Monday morning when they do not want to go to school. Salespeople suffering from call reluctance get it for virtually the same reason. Queasy stomach. Headache. Just not quite up to getting out and charging into a day of calling on strangers.

One more symptom of call reluctance is "celebration syndrome." It can be seen in the salesperson who makes a big sale in the morning and then celebrates by taking the rest of the day off or indulging in a three-hour lunch. The sales professional on an even keel would do just the opposite. The enthusiasm and satisfaction of a really big sale would make him or her want to jump right back in and make another sale, not go out and spend that commission check.

Finally, call reluctance can be seen in what is known as busywork. This is a lot like the problem of paperwork. However, it involves work *outside* the office instead of *inside* it. Examples include taking time out from the job of selling for such things as baby-sitting, running errands, getting the oil changed in the car, etc. You would not take off from a salaried job to do these things. You should not take off from the job of selling to do them either.

Call Reluctance: The Prevention and Cure

Since call reluctance is so deadly most sales professionals do their best to give it a wide berth. Armed with the knowledge of what call reluctance is and how it manifests itself, they are always on the lookout for its symptoms. Should call reluctance strike, there are a number of ways to prevent or cure it.

The best deterrent of call reluctance is pure determination and resolve. When you feel a wave of it coming on, crank up the self-discipline. Your alarm goes off at 6:00 and you want to roll over for just 15 more minutes. For the very reason that you *want* to sleep in, get out of bed then and there. Avoid debating with yourself about it. The issue is closed. Do it. Every day that you get up on time will make it that much easier to do the next day. On the other hand, every time you roll over and give in to yourself makes it that much harder. Be disciplined. Be tough. And make yourself take yourself seriously. In time, this will help you turn positive work actions into habits. And the more firmly these good habits are entrenched, the greater will be your own personal happiness and productivity, and the lesser will be the possibility of your falling under the spell of call reluctance. According to a well-known yet anonymous quotation:

> *Sow a thought, and you reap an act;*
> *Sow an act, and you reap a habit;*
> *Sow a habit, and you reap a character;*
> *Sow a character, and you reap a destiny.*

The most delightful thing about good habits is that, though they may start out in full rebellion, they eventually become good friends.

Another method for heading off call reluctance before it develops into a terminal case is to follow sound time management practices. Every successful sales professional maps out his or her objectives for the year, and then divides them by each month and, sometimes, each week. Focusing on clear objectives, the sales professional is then able to plan the kind of activity required to meet them. Then either the night before or early each morning, he or she lays out the entire day's activity. This technique divides and subdivides what may well be overwhelmingly huge plans into manageable, daily goals.

Famed motivator Dale Carnegie once observed that his wife must have washed thousands of dishes over the years. He asked her how she managed to go back to that sink every day. She explained that she never thought about the thousands of dishes she had washed in the past and the thousands she would wash during the years to come. She just concentrated on the ones right in front of her that day.

You should do the same in sales. Let's say you set your goal at 300 sales this year. That amount in itself is really beyond comprehension. But dividing it into 50 weeks means only six sales each week. And to accomplish that may require four sales calls each day. You know that's what it will take. So, each morning, you look at your daily activity sheet, see what you have to do, knowing that if you meet your daily objectives today and every day, you will have met your annual goal by the end of the year. By giving yourself this track to run on, these guidelines of daily objectives to follow, you will find they help motivate you out of a call reluctance slump. They will also help you level out inconsistencies in your productivity and keep you going on a sort of "automatic pilot" on days when you cannot seem to get your burners fired up. We will discuss time management in more detail in Chapter Three: "Selling as a Process."

The above suggestions — self-discipline and time management — help chase away call reluctance when it shows up at your door. But there are also long-term defenses, the best one being KNOWLEDGE! Knowledge breeds competence, which in turn leads to confidence. Imagine the feeling of confidence when, standing on a prospective buyer's doorstep, you begin to get a twinge of call reluctance. But then you remember that you know your product inside and out, you know how to present that product the best way possible, and you have a reasonably good idea what to expect from the prospect on the other side of that door. In other words, you know what you are doing. So you have no reason to hesitate.

Another surefire method of fending off call reluctance is to prepare for each interview. Never attempt to walk in cold. While all sales are similar, each is different enough to warrant individual preparation and a review of pertinent data already on hand. For a new salesperson, this may require a great deal of time, as you review your products, the fact situation as best you know it about the prospect, and the particular approach — virtually word for word — that you intend to use during the interview. As you become more experienced, preparation may consist of little more than a review of the prospect's file and running through a mental checklist of key points while driving to the appointment. Whatever it takes, the important thing to remember is that you should be ready for each interview.

Much of this goes back to putting yourself in the right frame of mind, gearing yourself mentally for the interview. This enables you to walk in prepared, with your mind on the sale. If possible, try to review the entire interview in your mind as you imagine it will take place. Explore every sales possibility and every possible objection. You may even find it wise to have one or two backup proposals ready, just in case. Then by the time you are ready for the interview, you really are ready. You have covered every point, anticipated every objection, mapped out your proposal, and closed the sale — before you have even entered the prospect's home or office. The only thing left to do now is to go on in, carry out the presentation as planned, and walk out with the sale.

The final — the ultimate — weapon against call reluctance is to believe in what you are doing. Believe in yourself, your career, your product. Be excited about what you do and what you sell to the point that you want to tell people about it. A sales professional is not by nature cool, calm and reserved. The sales professional, the *successful* sales professional is turned on by what he or she is doing, is motivated, is excited and ready to explode with the good news of what he or she has to offer prospects.

Selling as a Profession

Selling is a profession. And it is an honorable profession. It offers the rewards of unlimited income potential, freedom to direct and control the course of your own life, and rewards commensurate with your willingness to work. But selling is not easy. To be successful as a sales professional requires a great deal of hard work, self-discipline, self-motivation, an interest in people, a knowledge of those people, and the ability to organize your time and your work.

And that is the subject of Chapter Three, "Selling as a Process." In the following pages you will learn how to place selling in its true perspective. You will also learn about the concept of organized selling, both from the point of view of the organized sales presentation and the organized sales professional.

Chapter Three

Selling as a Process

In our society, we are taught to shoot for perfection, to do it right or not do it at all. We do not like to settle for half a loaf. If we cannot have it all, we do not want any of it. Because of that (possibly misguided) way of thinking, time and time again, potentially excellent salespeople walk away from success because they fail to recognize it as success. They ignore the fact that they may have made sales in 50% of their calls that day (in actuality an incredible closing ratio for anyone, especially a novice). Instead, they bemoan the fact that 50% got away, and think of themselves as failures.

One of my first experiences in sales was as a life insurance agent. I was given the rate book, a sales track to memorize and 15 minutes of instruction about the "whys" and "how-tos" of prospecting. I had never before sold anything and knew nothing about sales skills. I memorized the sales track, beat the bushes for prospects, and in less than three weeks managed to secure about 20 appointments, from which I made five sales, all with almost no supervision, no guidance, and very little assistance from my sales manager (who, by the way, was a great salesman and became a manager against his own better judgment). Anyhow, I felt like the world's greatest failure. After all, I had knocked myself out for three weeks and had managed to rack up only 20 measly appointments. Plus, I had only sold one out of every four of those, a less than 25% closing ratio.

I did not know I was not expected to close a sale on *every* appointment. I assumed I was a failure. But thinking back on it, I had been a total success. From a dead start, I had learned a sales presentation, managed to scare up a whole truckload of prospects (none of whom were relatives), get on the phone and obtain 20 appointments, and actually sold five policies. I had gotten off to a better start than most new agents, but I had not known it. I quit that position, not learning until some time later that I had been on the road to success all along.

What I had failed to learn was that nobody bats a thousand.

In major league baseball, if a player could get a hit every time he went to bat, he would be batting 1.000, a perfect batting average. It sounds simple enough. However, the best annual batting average in the major league in the 20th Century, was a mere .424, earned by Rogers Hornsby, with the St. Louis Cardinals, in 1924. For every 100 times Hornsby was at bat, he got a hit on the average only 42.4 times. That's less than half. But Rogers Hornsby holds the title for the best annual batting average!

It is the same in selling. Even the greatest professionals in the world do not make *every* sale. They may start with closing ratios of one out of seven or one out of eight. Over the years, as they improve their skills, they also improve their closing ratios. Eventually, they may be closing one out of two sales interviews or even better. But nobody makes every sale. And nobody should expect to do so.

Selling is a numbers game. In certain industries, it may require, on the average, ten prospects to yield three appointments to obtain one sale. This produces a prospects-appointments sales ratio of 10-3-1! For some individuals, those figures may vary. For a new salesperson, the figures may be *20-5-1*. For a savvy old veteran, they may be *5-2-1* or even 3-2-1. The point is that the concept of a decreasing ratio of prospects to appointments to sales holds true. And amazingly enough, those figures tend to remain fairly constant for new salespeople in a given industry.

For illustration purposes, let's look at that goal of 300 sales this year. Forget the dollar value of each. Just concentrate on the number of sales for now. Besides, it has been the experience of most sales professionals that if they concentrate on the number of sales they make, the average dollar value per sale will tend to increase by itself over time. Now let's assume that your company's records indicate that, on the average, it takes a new salesperson ten prospects to obtain three interviews to make one sale. In other words, the sales ratio is 10-3-1.

In order to make your yearly sales objective, you will need 3,000 names, which will yield 900 appointments. That's a lot. But it is far from impossible. And if that is the *average* for new salespeople, there is no reason why you cannot meet or beat that number. You just have to start looking at selling as a process. That is the secret (magic, knack, trick, whatever you want to call it) to becoming a successful sales professional.

Selling as a Process

Remember what I said earlier. Products do not sell themselves, and they rarely sell by accident. They are sold by trained sales professionals. It is true that, given enough time and a lot of luck, anybody could sell something at least once. But to be successful in sales means to get out and sell, day in and day out. And though you are going to work hard if you are to become successful, you should also learn how to work smart. You can wander the streets hoping a sale will fall in your lap or you can plan a success course and stick to it. You can learn to do things efficiently.

For instance, go back to that example of 300 sales. Meeting that goal means you need 3,000 prospects. You are not going to find them by accident. It will require a plan, a prospecting system that consistently produces the number of prospects you regularly need. It will also require a great deal of planning to be able to see 900 of those prospects in that year in order to garner those 300 sales. But when you look at selling as a process, the attainment of that goal is not only possible, but it is highly probable.

First, think of the sales process as you would a factory or an assembly line.

Your prospects are the raw material that go in one end. During the sales process, those raw prospects are refined into several actual appointments. Finally, the appointments, through the sales process, are converted into an even smaller number of highly valuable sales.

Once you have the sales process in proper perspective, the next step is to reduce the year's objectives into numbers with which you can effectively deal. Those 300 sales a year mean just 25 sales per month, or just about six per week. Nobody can make 300 sales in a year. But most people could make six in a week. That is just one per day (if you work Saturdays).

Now, the idea is to make sure you keep that assembly line process moving. If you are like most salespersons, you love to sell, but you hate to prospect. However, if you stop prospecting, or cut back too much, appointments will begin to dry up. Then sales will drop off. Maintaining the numbers you need at every point is necessary to keep the entire process humming along like a well-oiled machine, or like the assembly line it actually is.

This all sounds simple. And admittedly, it's easier said than done. So, the big question is — *how?* How do you turn the theory about a process into a reality?

If you are going to get the names of 60 good prospects each week, if you are going to set up 18 appointments each week, if you are going to make those six sales each week, you need a plan. You must be organized. You cannot wake up every morning and decide, "Maybe I'll prospect a little or maybe I'll see if I can get a couple of appointments."

	Prospects	Appointments	Sales
Per Year	3,000	900	300
Per Month	250	75	25
Per Week	60	18	6

You have to take that big process and divide it into smaller processes: a prospecting process, an appointment-getting process, a sales process, and so on. You will be supervising a number of processes. To do all that — to do it well — the first step is to start thinking like an independent businessperson.

The Sales Professional as a Business Person

Managing a sales career is, in many respects, like running a factory or an assembly line. More specifically, selling *is* running a business. And as a sales professional, you must realize that you are, in almost every respect, a self-employed business person. As was discussed earlier, you enjoy the freedom of being your own boss, in that you pretty much set your own hours, make out your own schedule, watch your own expenses and keep your own records. That sounds very much like an independent business owner. And to assure your success, you must learn to think like one, to conduct your affairs like one. You must *be* an independent business owner. This means you must become something of an expert in some very important business and sales related areas. They are: Goal Setting; Record Keeping; and Time Management

1. Goal Setting

What do you intend to accomplish this year? Where do you want to be five years from now?

Setting out to do something without clear objectives is like going on a long trip without any idea where you are going or how you plan to get there. If you do not have clear goals, you'll simply end up wandering in circles. You will never know where you are, where you have been, or where you are going. If you end up someplace worth being, you will have done so purely by accident.

As a businessperson, setting clear, realistic objectives is the first and perhaps the most important step to becoming successful. That is because it is the first step to becoming organized. Avoid being like people who simply strive, not knowing what it is they are even hoping to achieve or attain. Perhaps you have seen them. They may work hard enough for two or three people. But they do not know where they are going. And in the end, they literally go nowhere. They are so busy working that they have not taken the time to plan *where* that work will lead them, let alone figure out the best way to get there.

That's the difference between working *hard* and working *smart*. Working smart means you may be able to accomplish more in five hours than others might get done in twice that time. Merely putting in time will not make you a success (remember, as a commissioned sales professional you do not receive a commission check for just going through the motions of being productive). The only way to begin working smarter is to know exactly what you want to accomplish each day, each week, each month. And that means you must have goals.

Every year, well-run businesses — from small one-owner establishments to multibillion-dollar corporations employing hundreds of thousands of workers — undertake a planning process during which they set one-year, three-year, and five-year goals. Once these goals are set, every resource is bent toward attaining them. Their goals quite literally chart the course of the business. They are the purpose of the business. Actions that bring the company closer to these goals are carried out. Others, which do not contribute, are eliminated.

As an independent businessperson, you must do the same thing. Start by setting your annual sales goals, be they dollar totals or numbers of sales. This simple task alone will tend to point to the actions necessary to realize those goals. For instance, do you value industry awards or recognition? If so, set your sights on them. Which ones? Be specific. Then go beyond your business goals to your personal goals. What do you want out of life? A bigger house? The ability to pay for your children's college educations? A second honeymoon to Bermuda? Retirement at age 60? A happy home life? Whatever you want, take some time *today* to set your own goals. The several hours you spend will pay off a hundredfold.

How do you begin? When it comes to goals and then meeting them, there are three things you must do. First, write them down on paper. Do not just think about them. Put them in black and white. That makes them more real to you and less likely to change slowly over time. Second, be as specific as possible. Do not write, "I want to be rich," or "I want to make a lot of sales." Instead, phrase your goals like this: "I want to be worth a million dollars in net assets," or "I want to make 250 sales." Third, set deadlines. Unless you decide upon a date by which you intend to accomplish each goal, there is a good chance you will not take the necessary action to make it a reality. Vaguely worded goals, with no imposed deadlines, rarely add up to anything more than wishes that never come true. So, your goals may read, "I want to be worth a million dollars in net assets by age *50,*" or "I want to make 250 sales by December 31 of this year."

In his book *Staying Ahead of Time,* noted author and time management expert, Dr. Dennis Hensley, advocates creating what he calls a "Life Map." This "Life Map" helps you put down in black and white where you intend to be one, three, five, 15 and 30 years from now.

You should develop your own life map, fill it in, and then keep it in front of you, located prominently in your line of sight on the wall by your desk. You may even wish to frame it. Above all, do *not* simply fill it out and file it away where it can be forgotten.

Life Map

Write a Who's Who Entry About
Your Life and Accomplishments to be presented by a loved one at your
retirement dinner:

Achievement Date:

===================================

Do the same for the following dates:

Thirty Years From Now
Achievement Date:

Fifteen Years From Now
Achievement Date:

Five Years From Now
Achievement Date:

Three Years From Now
Achievement Date:

One Year From Now:
Achievement Date:

Another device recommended by Dr. Hensley is the "Time Management
Contract" between you and yourself to meet one or more objectives by a
given date. By drafting such a contract, you elevate your goals to more than

just ideas. To help insure that you fulfill your half of the contract, distribute copies to a select few people for safekeeping. Make sure that these are people who care about you and understand what you are doing. And ask them periodically to touch bases with you regarding how you are coming along. In other words, ask them to both gently encourage you and also act as nagging hair shirts, depending on which will help produce the best results.

Once you have established your goals for today, for next month, for this year, for the next three years, and beyond — look at them *every* day. Make them your guiding force. Keep them uppermost in your mind. Set your will, your talents, all your efforts toward attaining them. Quite often, the very existence of clear goals themselves will subconsciously stimulate your mind toward attaining them, and will sometimes even indicate the very action needed to do so. By the mere act of setting goals, half your planning task is completed.

==

Time Management Contract

I, (full name), agree to accomplish each of the following items on or before (target date) and thereby do formally contract myself to these purposes. These goals are challenging, but reasonable, and I accept them willingly.

(A)

(B)

(C)

(D)

(E)

Signed by: _____ Date: _____

===

Remember the goal of 300 sales in a year. Simply by setting that annual goal, your mind begins seeking ways to attain it.

With solid, carefully thought-out goals before you, half your job is done. Without goals, it is difficult to determine even what that job is, let alone get it done.

2. Record Keeping

Goals give your life purpose, both as an individual and as a sales professional. They point to where you want to be next week, next year, the next decade. But how do you know when you have attained your goals? How do you know if you have missed them? How do you determine where you are at any given point in time? The answer is simple. You must keep records.

Goals tell you what you would like to accomplish. Records tell you how well you are accomplishing them. Records provide you with feedback. Once a ship's course is set, the navigator, using charts, compasses and other navigational equipment, can determine its precise location at any point in time. In baseball, statistics and record keeping are almost a mania ("Bobby averages .239 against left-handed, squint-eyed pitchers in games played on Thursdays"). Every business calculates the cost of operation compared to the cost of sales. Records. Records. Records. They are more than important. They are vital for the success of any venture, any goal. And they are vital if you are going to be successful as a sales professional.

What does good record keeping do? First and foremost, it helps you plan. Remember those prospects-appointments-sales ratios I discussed earlier? They are the result of careful record keeping. Say you started your sales career on January 1st. From the very first day, you recorded every business-related detail. On one sheet of paper, you wrote down the number of prospects you acquired every day, and basic details about each (income, age, address, etc.). On another sheet, you kept track of the number of appointments. On a third sheet, you recorded complete data on every sale (age of buyer, income of individual or business, size of the sale, etc.). Then on December 31st, you took all your raw figures (realistically, you would probably do this every month) and found that you had acquired the names of 2,450 prospects during the year. Of those, 637 (or 26%) granted you appointments; and 250 (or approximately 39% of the 637) purchased a product from you.

You could thus determine that, for you, the ratio of prospects-appointments-sales is 2,450-637-250 or approximately 10-2.5-1. These figures show that, for every ten prospects, you are averaging one sale.

How you keep your records and the detail to which you keep them are up to you. Your company may have planning and record keeping forms to use. Most preprinted forms do quite well, enabling you to track your goals and chart your progress for one year. Keep records of the pertinent information both you and your sales manager agree you need. Track as much information and in as much detail as you feel is necessary.

Fortunately, with computer programs available, you can track and analyze a multitude of variables and factors. For instance, you can often determine where the majority of your sales come from. If 65% of your business comes from prospects who earn between $75,000 and $100,000 a year and are in the health care industry, you can then either (A) focus all your activities in this market or (B) explore how to expand into other markets. The choice is yours.

At the very minimum, track the number of prospects (along with data on their case size, location by relevant area, income, pertinent personal information, where you obtained the names, etc.), number of appointments (along with pertinent data here, too), number of sales, characteristics of each buyer, size of each sale, how long it took you to make the sale from prospecting to closing, and commission per sale. Also track basic expenses, including cost of each cancellation, cost of driving to and from appointments, and time spent on the road. This is the bare minimum. And it really does not take long to record this information every day. More and more sales professionals are doing their record keeping on computer. With proper programming, a computer can provide you with a daily standing of how well you are doing, and only take you minutes each day.

While we're on the subject, a word of warning is appropriate: though detailed record keeping is important, do not become obsessed by it. Records are a means of checking your progress toward your goals. They should not become goals themselves. Most successful sales professionals devote no more than half an hour each day to record keeping and daily planning. At the end of the week, perhaps on a Friday or Saturday afternoon when things are winding down, they may take an hour or two to examine the week's activity, look for any problem areas, and then plan the coming week's work. Once a month, they bring all the weekly totals up to date. Finally, in December (or whenever they schedule their year-end), they set aside several days to do an analysis of the entire year and establish the next year's goals. Most of all, do not get sidetracked from prime selling time to do record keeping.

3. *Time Management*

There is a great deal of truth to the old saying that "time is money." And it should be increasingly obvious to you, as a sales professional, that it takes a great deal of planning and organizing to get you in front of the right type and the right number of prospective buyers each day. There are a lot of things you must do, and there are only 24 hours each day in which to do them. In those 24 hours, you have to devote time to prospecting, to planning, to self-education, to record keeping, to balancing the books, and to maintaining your personal and home life as well. Oh, and don't forget selling! All this means is that you have to become something of an efficiency expert.

As a sales professional, time is your greatest resource, your most valuable asset. But time is also a funny thing in that it is a limited asset. As Dr. Hensley notes: "Everyone has the same 24 hours each day, 168 hours per week. The wealthy person is given no more time than the poor person, the old person is given no more time than the young person and the efficient user of time is given no more time than the time waster." It is not the number of hours we have, but the qualitative use we make of these hours. Dr. Hensley is a living example of his own words. By age 35, he had served a tour of duty in Vietnam, survived a crippling disease which left him partially paralyzed for six months, earned a doctoral degree, published over 2,250 articles in a wide range of magazines and academic journals, written four books, earned a reputation as one of the top Jack London scholars in the world, and been voted "Best Motivational Speaker" in a nationwide survey of Christian writers.

And he hasn't slowed up yet. Today, he is founder and director of the Professional Writer's Program at Taylor University at Fort Wayne and, at last count, has published more than 50 books. He has accomplished all these things and still always found time to devote to his wife, children, grandchildren, and church.

The point is that, while time is a limited resource, a person who understands time and wants to capitalize on it can virtually expand it into limitless dimensions through effective time management. Again, the idea is to learn to work smarter, not just harder. If you have your goals clearly before you and have organized your time and your mind, you can accomplish phenomenal things. Think in terms of objectives and accomplishments, not numbers of hours. Do not brag, "I put in 65 hours this week." Say instead, "I saw 30 potential buyers this week, and I closed 15 of them."

I used to work no less than six and a half days a week. I felt guilty if I was not working. Even on that half day when I was not "putting in time" (which in retrospect is really what it was), I was distracted, thinking about work. Then someone told me about a theory which advocates that you expand the task to fill the time. In other words, if you allot five hours to complete a certain task, you will finish in five hours. But if you allow yourself ten hours, the task will take ten hours. I decided to test the theory myself, because I was getting sick of working all the time and getting no further ahead than my friends and associates who were putting in banker's hours. So, I started budgeting my time, planning for a five-day week. That next week, I accomplished in 50 hours tasks that would have required 65 hours the week before. And I treated myself to my first guilt-free weekend off in years.

Since then, I have learned to control time, and make it work for me. I have harnessed a resource that I had previously believed to be totally out of my control. And the results have been amazing. I not only have more (and more enjoyable) time for family, friends and church, but I consistently accomplish more of my objectives in less time than I would have thought possible before I learned the art of time management.

Let's say you are willing to put in 40 hours a week building your career. And up to now, you have accomplished a designated week's worth of work in those 40 hours. Let's also say that a week's work usually earns you $1,500, making each hour worth $37.50. Assume that, through effective time management, you are now able to get that week's work done in 35 hours. You have raised the value of an hour's worth of work from $37.50 to nearly $43 ($42.86 to be exact). Plus, you have five new "found" hours a week. That's another 250 hours a year, or an additional 35 seven-hour days at your disposal.

Through effective time management, which added one more productive hour a day, five more a week, you now have a 13.5-month year, while the rest of the world has only 12. What can that mean in terms of earnings? Well, the old 40-hour week (with each hour worth *$37.50)* earned you $1,500. In a 50-week year, total earnings would be $75,000. Now you have a 40-hour week with each hour worth $42.86. Each week you can expect to average $1,714.40, for an annual total of $85,720. You have just increased your annual income by $10,220 by working the same number of hours. That's what is meant by the term, "work smarter, not harder."

Just about every successful person has learned the art of time management, and has learned how to use time to his or her advantage. You can do the same. In fact, if you are to be successful, you *must* do the same. It is not as difficult as you might think. If you have done a proper job of setting your goals and have adopted a workable record keeping system, you know what you have to do each week to stay on target. Let's demonstrate by looking at our previous example of a 300-sales-per-year goal. Using a 50-week year, you would need 60 prospects to obtain 18 appointments to make six sales each week. The example below shows how a typical week might look.

Weekly Schedule

Monday
7:30- 8:30	Breakfast appointment with prospect (appt. #1)
8:30-12:00	Prospect (acquire at least 30 names)
12:00-1:00	Lunch appointment with prospect (appt. #2)
1:00-1:30	Paperwork
1:30-5:00	Call for next week's appointments (no less than 8)
5:00-5:30	Record day's results/review Tuesday's schedule

Tuesday
7:30- 8:30	Paperwork
8:30- 9:30	Appointment with prospect (appt. #3)
10:00-11:00	Appointment with prospect (appt. #4)
11:30-12:30	Lunch appointment with prospect (appt. #5)
1:00- 2:00	Appointment with prospect (appt. #6)
2:30- 5:00	Call for next week's appointments (no less than 6)
5:00- 5:30	Record day's results/review Wednesday's schedule

Wednesday
7:30- 8:30	Breakfast appointment with prospect (appt. #7)
9:00-10:00	Appointment with prospect (appt. #8)
10:30-11:30	Appointment with prospect (appt. #9)
12:00-1:00	Paperwork over lunch in office
1:30- 2:30	Appointment with prospect (appt. #10)
3:00- 4:00	Appointment with prospect (appt. #11)
4:30- 5:00	Call for next week's appointments (no less than 1)
5:00- 5:30	Record day's results/review Thursday's schedule

Thursday
7:30- 8:30	Paperwork
9:00-10:00	Appointment with prospect (appt. #12)

10:30-11:30	Appointment with prospect (appt. #13)
12:00-1:00	Lunch appointment with prospect (appt. #14)
1:30- 2:30	Appointment with prospect (appt. #15)
3:00- 4:00	Appointment with prospect (appt. #16)
4:30- 5:00	Call for next week's appointments (no less than 1)
5:00- 5:30	Record day's results/review Friday's schedule

Friday

7:30- 8:30	Breakfast appointment with prospect (appt. #17)
9:00-10:00	Appointment with prospect (appt. #18)
10:30-2:00	Prospect/working lunch (acquire at least 30 names)
2:00- 3:00	Call for next week's appointments (no less than 2)
3:00- 5:30	Clean up week's paperwork, record week's results, review next week's schedule.

==

All it consists of is a detailed plan of each day's major activities, along with a time for each. By careful planning, a schedule such as this will enable you consistently to attain daily and weekly goals, because it provides you with a track upon which to run. You certainly will not need to wake up each morning and ask, "What shall I do today?" You will have it all laid out before you.

But perhaps you are the type of person who looked at that sample schedule and shook your head. "It's not for me," you thought. "I can't become a slave to such a schedule." If you feel that way, then you fail to understand the concept of time management, which is simply that you plan your time and devote yourself fully to the immediate task at hand, thereby *freeing* your time for other things. The schedule you use must be *your* schedule; it must reflect *your* objectives and goals. It should serve you, not the other way around.

Make Time Management Work for You

How can you begin applying the concepts of time management to your life and your career? First, study the subject. Though in these pages sufficient attention cannot be given this subject, there are other books devoted exclusively to time management.

But even before you start further study, you can begin applying the principles of effective time management *immediately.* Here is how. Today and tomorrow, keep a pad of paper and a pen or pencil with you at all times. Record or log *everything* you do, along with the time you spend doing it. Do not leave out such things as jawboning with friends, watching TV or reading the newspaper. Be honest. What you are doing is record keeping. The data you collect will help you provide you with an idea of how you spend your time.

Tomorrow evening look over your two-day list. How much time (rounded off to the nearest 15 minutes) did you spend doing constructive things? (Let's treat reading this book as a constructive activity.) How much time did you waste? Really study the figures. Now ask yourself, "How might I have saved time, or used my time more wisely?" Figure out how many hours you could have saved if you had wanted to. Finally, draft a schedule of what you plan to do on the third day.

Steps in the Sales Process: An Overview

In this chapter we have discussed the concept of selling as a process and the role of the sales professional as a businessperson. The remainder of this book is devoted to the universal process of selling: not only to what it is and how it works, but also to teaching how it can be applied successfully to a professional sales career.

As was mentioned earlier, you should learn to think of the sales process as an assembly line. We also discussed how each sale is virtually identical with all others in terms of the steps involved. Although many people have used a number of different ways to describe the sales process and some divide it into three steps or five steps (I have used seven), the principles are still the same. These steps will always include:

1. Prospecting.
2. Obtaining the appointment (including pre-approach).
3. The approach or introduction.
4. Identifying needs or problems.
5. Recommending your solution.
6. Closing the sale.
7. Providing follow-up and service.

The rest of this book will focus on these seven steps. . and will teach you how to utilize them in the sales process to insure your own success as a sales professional.

Chapter Four

Prospecting

Prospecting is not something you get out of the way so that you can get down to the job of selling. Prospecting is a *part* of selling, a very important part. In fact, it is the first step in the sales process.

To be effective, your prospecting efforts must become an ongoing activity, a process whereby you maintain a steady flow of prospective buyers to talk to about your products. Never underestimate the importance of prospects and the prospecting process. *Prospects are the raw materials from which sales are made.* Think of a company that manufactures, let's say, steel products. It has well-trained people, highly qualified managers, the most modern, efficient machinery and plants. But if the iron ore shipments are halted, or if the deliveries of coal to heat the furnaces are interrupted, the whole operation stops dead in its tracks. It cannot go on. How can it? The raw materials the company uses to make its products are not available.

The situation is similar for you in that, regardless of how well you understand your products, regardless of how effective you are at identifying and explaining a person's needs, regardless of how good you are at answering objections and closing sales, if you do not have the raw materials — if you do not have the prospects — you do not have any sales.

Prospecting Is a Process

Prospecting has a real image problem. For some reason, people equate it with endless hours of fruitless phone calls, wasted gas, dead ends. They think of doors slamming in their faces, disinterest, hostility and headaches. Prospecting receives that unfavorable image from salespeople who fail to understand that prospecting, like every other aspect of the sales cycle, is —

you guessed it — nothing more than a *process*.

However, for these prospecting haters, prospecting for likely buyers is more of a hit-or-miss ordeal that they tackle only when they have scraped the bottom of their prospect file and have no choice but to go out and track down a new batch of warm bodies. For these salespeople, prospecting is a miserable, frustrating, time-consuming, anxiety-ridden experience. They use trial-and-error tactics (if you could refer to their attempts as tactics at all) and a great deal of luck to secure the names of enough people to get by. It's no wonder these poor people hate prospecting. And you will too, if that's the way you do it.

However, prospecting can be carried out in an orderly, systematic manner, in such a way that — believe it or not — most successful sales professionals find to be rewarding and enjoyable. That is because they know what they are doing. They plan. They organize. They see prospecting as simply the first step in the sales process. And they see prospecting as a process in itself.

The process of prospecting has three steps. These are:

1. Deciding who your prospects are.

2. Selecting an approach to obtaining the names of prospects.

3. Actually obtaining the names and as much qualifying information as possible.

What Makes a Prospect a Prospect?

Let's first look at the process of identifying prospects, or determining what makes a prospect a prospect. So, what is a prospect? In spite of the characterization of every person in our society as a *consumer*, not every consumer is a prospect for every product or service. In other words, there is no single set of characteristics that describes a universal prospect. A prospect for one industry or product may not be a prospect for another. An athlete may be a prime prospect for a new type of running shoe, but not for a high-intensity weight-training program. A small company may make an ideal prospect for an overnight postal delivery service; however, it may not be a good candidate for the purchase of a fleet of delivery trucks. A young couple with small children may be prospects for high amounts of low-cost term life insurance, but not for a high-premium Variable Adjustable Life policy.

There is no such thing as a universal prospect. However, there is an ideal or optimum prospect for *each* product or service or industry or geographic area. These are the people or companies *most* likely to buy your products. Your task is to determine the ideal or best prospect for you and your products and gear your entire prospecting and sales activity toward that market.

How can you identify the ideal prospect? Well, in some industries it is a natural, self-completing process. If your company manufactures computerized engine parts for small airplanes, your market consists of companies that manufacture or service small airplanes. Or if your firm specializes in producing portable medical facilities for Third World developing nations, your natural markets may be oil-producing African or Asian nations or politically stable South American countries. In other words, if your product is fairly specialized, so will your market tend to be. These are what are known as natural markets: Rolls Royces for multimillionaires. Disposable diapers for parents of newborns. Educational textbooks for schools. And so on. On the other hand, the more general the appeal of your product, the greater the challenge to identify and select the ideal market.

This book cannot tell you what your ideal market is. However, it can teach you how to find it. If the process could be reduced to a mathematical formula, there would be four factors that would be taken into consideration. These are:

Product/Service Characteristics
+
Prospect Profile
+
Your Experience or Interests
+
Analysis of Your Records
= Your Ideal Market

First and foremost is the nature and design of your product, its characteristics. Most companies develop their products or services to meet a certain perceived need or with a certain group of consumers in mind. The market for homeowners or auto insurance policies is rather obvious, as is that for manufacturers of infants' clothes.

The second factor involves the characteristics or profile of potential prospects. You must develop a set of "ideal" characteristics. Factors to consider may include: age, income, marital status, profession, geographic location (a seller of jumbo jets may find Paris or Saudi Arabia a reasonable trip, while an insurance agent may not find it profitable to work outside of his or her county), numbers available (a potential prospect list of one million is a lot better than one of only 100), sex, interests or hobbies, and, for businesses, type of business structure, nature of the business, number of employees, and more.

A third factor takes into account your own interests and experience. What is your background? Who do you like working with? W. Clement Stone and Napoleon Hill, authors of *Success Through a Positive Mental Attitude,* tell a true story of an insurance salesman who liked nothing better than to spend weeks at a time tramping about in the woods. He got tired of working 50 weeks in the city in exchange for two weeks in the Great Outdoors, so he sold his house, packed his gear, and went to Alaska, where he built his career selling life insurance to the men and women working in the oil fields and along the Alaskan pipeline.

You too may have interests that will help you select your ideal market. Look first to what you know or have done in the past, as well as what you enjoy. For example, one of my "products" is marketing seminars. While I will talk to just about anyone, my ideal market (the one I enjoy the most) consists of small-business owners and non-profit organizations, especially religious groups. Why? Mostly because, as a small-business owner and entrepreneur myself, I love and understand the way business owners think and work. As for the nonprofit and religious groups, this also appeals to my interests. I am comfortable with each of these types of prospects, enjoy working with them, and, as a result, am successful with them.

Let your previous experiences and your interests help you select your ideal market. Perhaps it is a matter of age; you would prefer working with people your own age. Many insurance companies encourage new agents to concentrate on their peers. Not only is it fairly easy for them to establish rapport, but they are able to grow with their prospects. A 25-year-old agent may focus on young married couples with small children. As these men and women improve their lot financially, being promoted or forming their own businesses, the agent grows also. So, previous experience and interests are important.

At the same time, ask yourself where you want to go. Who you would like to have as your prospects is also important. The ability to constantly upgrade the quality of your prospects is an important part of your growth as a sales professional. As you become more experienced, more confident, you may want to upgrade your market from small sole proprietorships and partnerships with fewer than five employees to corporations employing up to 50 people or more. The point is that personal interest, previous experience, and future plans should be factors in your decision.

Finally, do not ignore your own records. Go with the flow. If they indicate that one-eyed sailors are your best prospects, direct more of your prospecting efforts in that direction.

Now, let's see if we can identify *your* ideal market based on these factors. Take a few minutes now and fill in the blanks in the box, Finding Your Ideal Market. Try to be as specific as possible.

Finding Your Ideal Market

Your Product/Service (For whom is it designed?)

Prospect Profile (Describe the characteristics of the most likely prospects)

Your Experience/Interests

Your Records (If you are new in sales and have no records, ask your sales manager for any available industry records)

Conclusions. My ideal market appears to be (Describe):

Mapping Out Your Strategy for Obtaining Names

Once you have zeroed in on your ideal prospect, the next step in the prospecting process is to map out the best approach to obtain names of specific prospects. Remember, prospecting must be done systematically if you are to reach your full potential as a sales professional. It is something you will do on a daily basis, as an integral part of the sales process. You know who your prospects are. Now, how do you reach them? Prospecting in a random, haphazard manner will prove to be time-consuming, inefficient and costly — *because the more time you are required to spend prospecting, the less time you will have for selling.*

There are several approaches to prospecting. Each has its place, the effectiveness of any one being dependent upon market, type of product you offer and other like factors.

Advertising

Advertising is the ideal method for businesses with products which meet an obvious consumer need or which are "hot" items, such as cars, high-technology products (computers, video games, digital cameras), household appliances, real estate, etc. Advertising gets the word out. And it works. If you have any doubts, pick up your local newspaper. A lot more space is devoted to advertisements than to news stories. Between radio, TV, newspapers, magazines and even billboards, businesses spend billions of dollars each year trying to attract prospective buyers.

The obvious advantage to advertising is that it brings the prospects to you. Of course, effective advertising depends on the nature of the product, the media selected, the quality and design of the ad piece, and the desire for the product as the market perceives it. While a professional ad can boost business, an amateurish one can do more damage than good. It is usually best to work with an advertising agency to develop material. However, that can run into a major expense. Also, advertising is simply not effective in some industries.

Typically, for the above reasons and unless in retail sales, the sales professional should proceed with caution when using media advertising as a prospecting method. The best rule of thumb is to talk to others in your industry about the results of advertising. If they recommend it, you may want to investigate further. If not, steer clear, at least until you are more established. Then — relying primarily on prospecting methods with better-proven effectiveness — you may wish to experiment with advertising on a supplemental basis.

Cold Calling

Cold calling is a more active prospecting approach compared to advertising. It is often looked down upon because it is equated with old-fashioned door-to-door selling. However, cold calling — when carried out with planning and forethought within a focused market — can be a highly effective means of obtaining quality prospects. That is because cold calling, in spite of its reputation, rarely involves going door-to-door these days. Yes, if you have an hour or two on your hands unexpectedly (perhaps a prospect cancels an appointment) and are near several potential prospects, drop by and introduce yourself. But a better use of cold calling as a *regular* prospecting method is to obtain membership lists of associations and organizations pertinent to your markets: the local Chamber of Commerce, country clubs, professional associations, industry associations, and so on. A financial planner targeting physicians may obtain the membership roster of the local chapter of the American Medical Association. A seller of restaurant supplies may obtain the National Restaurant Association list. Virtually every industry has at least one nationwide association representing its members.

Go online and surf the net for about ten minutes, and you will probably have list of organizations longer than your arm. (More on this below, when we talk about networking.)

Dun & Bradstreet, the prestigious company which tracks the activity of virtually *every* business in the nation, can provide detailed information on any company in your area by size, income, zip code, or just about any criteria. Don't overlook the phone book either. I know at least one insurance agent who keeps a White Pages in his desk drawer. If he finds himself with five or ten minutes of free time or comes up short of prospects from other sources, he grabs his phone book and simply starts calling. In one year, he had gone halfway through the A's in a major metropolitan area. And he has picked up enough new clients to make this tactic worth continuing on a fill-in basis. The Yellow Pages are equally good, since they categorize every business with a listed phone number. A quick glance through the Yellow Pages will reveal a ready list of prospects, whether you market to hypnotists or attorneys, construction companies or green houses, printing companies or restaurants. And most Yellow Pages even list businesses by area.

Cold calling does have its place. However, it is usually a low-return prospecting method. You know virtually nothing about the people you are contacting. Not only are they going to be somewhat reluctant to grant you an appointment, but you also have very little information to go on. And the less data you have about a prospect, the greater the odds of not coming home with an appointment. So, while cold calling does work, and is an ideal prospecting method in some areas and in some situations, it is generally less effective and less efficient than the next method of prospecting we will look at.

Networking

Especially with the internet, you have the potential to build relationships and contacts with people anywhere in the world. Cultivate and nurture such relationships. How? On line, identify websites and blogs of individuals, organizations companies. Chat with them, leave comments on their articles, and be sure to include your website address in your signature. (Note: Only leave positive comments. Some people cannot resist correcting and criticizing others. Avoid that. If a comment is especially off target, simply begin your comment with: "Another point worth bringing up is...."

But the real power of networking is to combine online relationship building with personal networking. The more people you know, and the more people you can help, the better a reputation you will build...and the more potential for business.

How can you make networking work for you? Well, used to be that networking meant you joined the Rotary and golfed at the country club, got together at the meet-and-greet cocktail hour to swap business cards and, almost as an afterthought, mentioned what you do for a living to your son's friend's father in the bleachers at the softball game.

Well, networking has grown up, mostly thanks to the internet, and it is one of the most effective, cost-effective ways for us small business owners to promote ourselves.

Think of networking as mostly free, word-of-mouth, marketing-by-walking-around. Here are some ideas to make networking work for you.

- **Be in touch.** Thanks to email, it's never been easier to stay connected with associates, clients and prospects from around the world. I send out short business and motivational tips via email on a regular basis. It's not uncommon for a client to click "reply" to talk about a new project. At the very least, everyone knows who I am and how to contact me.

- **Be involved.** Join organizations in your virtual and local business community. As a business consultant, I volunteer my time and talents with such organizations as NEW North in Northeast Wisconsin and the Kewaunee County Economic Development Council. Nationally, I provide marketing and communications support to an organization I helped found that represents my primary markets. Plus, I am involved in communications with Monarch Cursillo, a leadership and faith-building organization in the Episcopal Diocese of Fond du Lac in Wisconsin. The friendship and business connections are invaluable.

- **Polish your elevator talk.** Be prepared to tell someone who you are and what you do in the time it takes to take a 30-second elevator ride. Better yet, put your talk on the back of your business card.

- **Promote others...no strings attached.** Don't contact associates only when you want something. Be generous with your time. I recently had a local handyman, John Zellner, do some work on my property. His work was excellent, his price was fair, and his manner pleasant. I told the whole community. For an investment of 15 minutes (the time it took to compose an email), I sent out a strong endorsement of this gentleman to all my local contacts. Another way I promote others is to invite quality writers with a good message to contribute to my business blog (www.TheFreestyleEntrepreneur.com). This promotes them ... and helps promote my site and my business as well.

- **Send out calls for help.** When I need advice – whether I am seeking a recommendation for a good book to read or advice with a business problem – I send out an email to a very select group (the members vary depending on the topic) and ask them for help. The results are always amazing.

- **Be selective**. Don't waste your time on people with no talent, no work ethic or no understanding of the concept of a two-way relationship. Most of all, only endorse people you are confident can deliver. Recommending an unreliable associate will only reflect poorly on you.

- **Be limited.** Your job is not to be a bully pulpit. If you send out an email every week that heralds "the best (fill in the blank) I've ever met," pretty soon you'll get a reputation as a shameless promoter, and your messages will be deleted as spam.

- **Cultivate one-on-one relationships with good people.** A friend of mine, Bill Sheridan, from Iowa got me in the habit of scheduling 30-minute phone calls. I now do this (either monthly or quarterly) with about half a dozen business associates/friends. We talk about everything from business to our families to our faith to our troubles.

- **Invite three or four associates to become your board of directors.** These men and women may be outside your industry, but are key members of the community (either local or virtual). They may include your banker, president of the Chamber of Commerce, or just someone with integrity and wisdom. Meet quarterly over breakfast or via teleconference. Pick their brains and ask for advice on specific and general business situations. You pay them back by volunteering to serve on their boards, using their services and recommending them to others.

The bottom line: Networking works. It's inexpensive and builds business by building relationships, which makes it a perfect marketing tool for small-business owners. Make it work for you.

Referred Lead Prospecting

Referred lead prospecting is the Cadillac of prospecting techniques and is closely related to (some say it is a part of) networking. The concept is relatively simple. You acquire the names of new prospects — along with as much qualifying information as possible — from existing customers and clients or from centers of influence (more about them in a moment). In fact, referrers need not even be buyers. Regardless of whether or not a prospect buys, if you have made a respectable showing in the interview, there is no reason why you cannot ask for the names of other prospects. Referred lead prospecting is effective. Most of all, it is in referred lead prospecting that the concept of prospecting as an integral part of the sales process is most obvious. This is just one reason why referred lead prospecting is so valuable. Others include:

- Prospects may be approached on the most favorable basis possible, with a ready introduction as the friend of a friend or business acquaintance. When you get on the phone and say, "Jennifer Brown at the Kewaunee County Economic Development Corporation mentioned your name," you begin with at least one thing in common — a mutual friend — and, by establishing familiarity, have just increased the odds of getting an appointment.

- Prospects may be qualified — at least to some degree — in advance. If you obtain as much pertinent information as you can about each prospect from the referrer, you go in well armed about possible needs. It also helps you eliminate the names of people who do not look like good prospects. Most of all, you can zero in more effectively on your target market and stay within that market of "ideal" prospects. For example, if your ideal prospect is a closely held business, remember that business owners often deal with others of their kind. Because they share many of the same problems and concerns, they sometimes gravitate toward each other when at social or business gatherings. Even competitors in the same industry are often on friendly terms and are often willing to help each other out, and will gladly pass along a name to you. In fact, they are quite knowledgeable about each other's affairs. The result for you is *prospecting control.* If you know the type of prospects you want, referred lead prospecting can produce them.

- Because it is so effective, referred lead prospecting is a proven time saver, allowing you to devote more of your time and effort selling, and less prospecting. For every one appointment you obtain through hours of cold calling, you may get as many as five or six through referred leads gained in just one interview.

- Referred lead prospecting helps instill a sense of confidence not only in your chances of gaining appointments, but also in your abilities as a salesperson. After all, you probably wouldn't have been able to get the referral in the first place had the referrer any reason to question your capabilities. The confidence you feel, in turn, is communicated to prospects and clients.

- Finally, referred lead prospecting contributes to increased production, primarily because it produces more and better prospects than other methods.

There are two ways to undertake referred lead prospecting: through centers of influence or through what is known as the endless chain approach. Most people use a combination of both. I include them below as individual prospecting methods. However, as should be becoming evident, most prospecting methods do overlap.

Centers of Influence

Centers of influence are people who are able to provide you with names of prospects on a regular basis. They are often in key positions, such as the presidency of an organization or they are in charge of — or at least have access to — membership rosters. For example, a friendly banker or CPA, without divulging any privileged information, can provide the names of businesses that are expanding their operations. A real estate salesperson can provide you with information about people moving into certain neighborhoods, the neighborhoods in which most of your ideal prospects reside. This is also why networking is so important and valuable.

Centers of influence often make good members of your board of directors. Ideally, centers of influence should:

1. Be favorably well known in their communities or spheres of activity.

2. Be favorably well-disposed to both you and your products and services.

3. Be good prospectors themselves; understand, basically, the definition of a "qualified" prospect and alert to changing situations of their acquaintances.

4. Be joiners — gregarious enough to belong to organizations where they have exposure to people.

How can you develop centers of influence? Make a list of people who, because of their occupations or their professions, know a great many of the right kind of people. It is not difficult for you to get to know these people better. If you will become interested in their work, if you will volunteer your services in connection with some special community work in which you know they are interested, if you will go out of your way to meet them at the right time and under the right conditions, you can develop the acquaintanceship to the point that it will be logical for you -- without strain or embarrassment -- to ask them to sponsor you to their friends and acquaintances. Regard your selected centers of influence as your silent partners, and then make them in deed and in truth your partners by building your relationship with them on a sound basis.

Endless Chain

The endless chain approach is the second way to prospect by referral. In theory, the endless chain means that you obtain prospects from each appointment, moving from prospect to sale to prospect, in an endless chain. And in reality, it works superbly. Many successful sales professionals have found that, by simply asking for five to ten names at the conclusion of each sales interview — whether or not a sale was made — they have more prospects than they could ever hope to contact . . . a delightful problem, to say the least!

How to Get Referrals

Whichever approach to getting referrals you favor, the process of making it work for you involves four steps:

1. *Prepare in advance.* Know how you are going to get those names before you walk in the door. Do not attempt to "wing it." Done properly, referred lead prospecting can pay off in a big way. But without forethought and planning, it wastes both your time and that of your buyers.

2. *Prepare the referrer for the request.* Once you have prepared yourself, the next step is to prepare the referrer. Explain early in the interview that you will be asking for names later. This not only gets the referrer thinking of names during the interview, but it also avoids catching him or her by surprise when it comes time for the actual request.

3. *Close the interview with the referral request.* Do not allow yourself to become sidetracked during the interview. After all, your primary

motive is to make a sale. Only after all business is concluded should you ask for the names of prospects. But at the same time, do not treat this part of the interview as an unimportant afterthought. Take it seriously and your referrer will take it seriously also. Take your time. You probably will not need more than ten minutes, but they are ten important minutes. When you make your request, choose your words carefully. Do not ask for the names of companies or individuals who the referrer feels might be good prospects for your products. Instead, ask for names of people or businesses which meet the characteristics of your ideal or target market: "Are there any other companies in town which do over 100,000 mailing pieces a year?" "Who else is a member of the association?" "Have any of your friends recently bought a house?"

4. *Obtain qualifying information.* Once you have a list of names, go back and gather as much data about those individuals or companies as possible. Remember, the more information you obtain, the better prepared you will be to approach each prospect. Start with the basics: full name, address, phone number, age, approximate income, marital status and occupation for individuals. If prospects are businesses, you will want slightly different information, with less emphasis on personal facts (except when the need is life insurance or financial planning). The objective is to obtain information that will help you get an appointment and prepare for a sale.

Prospecting by Seminars

A highly effective method of prospecting in the right markets involves the use of specialized seminars to targeted prospect groups on subjects of interest.

The advantages are many. If you do your job right, you have managed to make a lasting impression on a large number of prospects who see you as competent in your field, an individual to call on for advice. Many attendees think of themselves as clients before they even buy anything from you. The seminar sets you up as the expert, the one who has the answers. It also puts you in the catbird seat, so to speak, when you get on the phone within a day or two after the seminar to arrange appointments to talk to attendees on a one-on-one basis or send follow-up literature. If you have selected your audience carefully and have a good list of names with which to work, seminar prospecting can lead to more, better qualified prospects than you had imagined possible.

Elements of a Successful Seminar

- It is targeted to a select, specific group.

- It is informative, giving the attendees information of which they may not be aware, and which will be of interest to them.

- It both disturbs the attendees and motivates them to want to do something about what they have learned.

- It establishes you as a competent professional.

- It leads to individual appointments.

Setting up seminars via local business associations, I promote my consulting services through presentations to business owners. I try to provide quality information about a specific need (for example: "Branding," Big-time Marketing on a Small-time Budget," or "How to Make Networking Work"). Using newspaper ads and placement of brochures in salons and women's fitness spas, friends of mine host educational seminars on health to promote their hormone replacement therapy business.

Key to an effective seminar is that no actual selling takes place during the seminar itself. The purpose is to educate, inform (and sometimes disturb) attendees about common problems or concerns. Seminars may be relatively small in scale (a presentation to four or five prospects over coffee in your office) or a major event (cocktails and three-course dinner for 150 in a rented hall).

If you were to divide an effective seminar into its main components, you would find that it has three major units or parts:

- *Pre-seminar preparation*, which will require 90% of your time devoted to seminar prospecting. You must select and attract an audience, set up the location and room arrangements, and prepare your presentation.

- *The seminar itself, which may take anywhere* from two to three hours, the execution of which is critical to its success. This includes properly registering participants and socializing with them prior to the formal presentation, the actual presentation itself, along with questions and answers, followed by post-seminar mingling and handling informal, one-on-one questions.

- *Post-seminar follow-up*, which can be thought of as the payoff. After the seminar, the participants should be asked to evaluate in writing the seminar and indicate areas about which they may have additional questions. Finally, within a few days following your seminar, you should then contact each participant with a thank you note and invitation to a personal, one-on-one appointment.

The Challenge of Prospecting

Prospecting is one of the greatest challenges with which any sales professional must deal. How successful you are at prospecting has as much to do with your attitude as with your approach. If you accept prospecting as a part of the sales process and look upon it in a positive light, half the battle is won. At the same time, be sure and take an approach which works and which is most comfortable for you. I know one salesman who loves cold calling. He can go to a strange city, pick up a phone book and begin making appointments. Others prefer referred lead prospecting. Still others are developing an effective seminar selling approach, while others do the majority of their prospecting online.

It really does not matter which approach you select, as long as you design and use a systematic approach and as long as you do it! Prospect regularly, as part of your overall activity plan, not when the spirit moves you. If you do not take the time to develop quality prospecting habits, no matter how long you are in the business and no matter how successful you may feel you are, you will always be no more than a hair's breath away from failing. On the other hand, many sales professionals believe that, no matter how weak you are in the sales presentation, no matter how you may bungle any other phase of the sales process, if you know how to bring in a regular, steady, consistent flow of quality prospects, you will not only make it in this business, you will make it in a big way.

Chapter Five

Getting the Appointment

Once you have a list of qualified prospects safely in hand, the next step is to contact them and get appointments.

Of course, you can just march right over to your prospect's home or business. But what if he isn't there? Or can't see you? Or can spare only ten minutes? Or refuses to see you? You have spent time obtaining the names of prospects. Wouldn't it be best to approach them in such a way as to maximize your chances of obtaining an appointment as well? Walking in cold off the street, no matter how well you have qualified your prospect, smacks of the old door-to-door approach to selling — working hard, but not smart.

Remember, you are a businessperson, a professional. That means you set up appointments in a businesslike, professional manner. There are two standard approaches. The first is to send a pre-approach letter by mail or email, followed by a phone call. The second is to skip the letter and simply call. Each has its advantages and drawbacks. The first approach is probably the most effective in terms of building a solid prospects-to-appointments ratio. However, sending letters to every prospect can be costly and time consuming. At the same time, simply getting on the phone and calling prospects, without the benefit of a pre-approach, introductory letter, is quick. Many successful sales professionals believe that appointments lost by not sending pre-approach letters are more than made up in saved postage and additional time available for calling more prospects. Whatever your choice, here is how to apply these approaches.

Pre-Approach Letter

A pre-approach letter introduces you to the prospect. That way, when you make the follow-up phone call, you are not a complete stranger. The letter adds a degree of credibility to your call. Another purpose of the pre-approach letter is to arouse the prospect's interest, which will in turn help open the door to an appointment.

The letter can be sent by regular mail or by email. As stated above, regular mail can be more effective, primarily because it will receive at least some focused attention. However, there is the matter of time and postage costs. On the other hand, when using email, there is always the risk that it will be blocked as spam or deleted because you are not known to the prospect. (For this reason, if the prospect's name was provided by a referrer, it is recommended to put the referrer's name in the subject line of the email. It can be something as simple as: "Referred to you by John Doe.")

Bear in mind that the letter itself should not be used to attempt to sell anything. That is not its purpose. It should simply whet the prospect's appetite for more information about your product or service and you and provide some credibility, as well as a link to your website or that of your company.

The letter should be concise and clear, containing only one idea. It should briefly explain who you are and indicate the type of service or product you can provide. If the prospect is a referral, be sure to mention the name of the referrer in the opening. Indicate that you will be in touch shortly to arrange a mutually convenient time to get together. Or request some type of action, whether it be an email or postcard reply or a visit to your website. Then close the letter.

Finally, if you have something to enclose or attach, a value-added freebie, such as a newsletter or other information piece, perhaps linking it to your website, do so. A typical pre-approach letter may read like the following sample.

Sample Pre-Approach Letter

Dear _____

There's a terribly corny line I learned when I first entered this business. It goes like this: "Those who fail to plan...fail."

The only problem with that line is that it's not really a line. It's true. Take estate planning, for instance.

As one of the articles in the enclosed issue of my newsletter points out, "No, we can't take it with us...but we don't have to fork it over to the government, either." That means planning, knowing what you want and finding out how to achieve it.

Best of all, even a little bit of planning to make sure your estate planning ducks are in a row can save a great deal of money...money that can go to your heirs rather than to Uncle Sam.

What do I recommend? I invite you to a no-cost, no-obligation consultation. If you would please give me a call or drop me an email at XXXXXXXXXX, we can arrange a convenient time to meet to discuss your long-term objectives and review your options.

As I said -- No cost. No obligation. Just the quality service I promise -- and try very hard to deliver -- to all my clients.

Sincerely,

(Your Name)

Phoning for the Appointment — Ten Tips

Within several days or a week after sending the letter, follow up with a phone call and request the appointment. Since this is one of the most crucial steps of the sales process — if you strike out at this point, you will not get in front of the prospect, let alone make a sale — let's will review it in detail. The techniques that follow apply whether or not you sent a pre-approach letter.

Email etiquette:

Is a phone call always necessary? No. It is sometimes possible to follow up with an email, but this is usually only recommended with prospects you know personally.

On the other hand, many prospects will feel less threatened and more open to an appointment when using email.

Sample email follow-up:

Name_____

I'm following up on my recent message about my services to schedule an appointment (no more than 30 minutes is

> *all we will need) to review some of your objectives. Would Wednesday at 9:45 AM be good for you, or would Thursday at 4:15 PM be better?*
>
> *And if you have any questions, please let me know.*

Reminder: Correct use of the phone is an art. Just because you have used the phone all your life does not mean you necessarily know how to use it *correctly*. So, forget you ever saw a telephone before and be prepared to learn from scratch. Here are ten things to keep in mind whenever you pick up the phone:

1. *Be prepared.* Do not get on the phone and then decide what you will say to your prospect. The successful sales professional avoids "winging" it when at all possible. You should develop a telephone sales talk and then learn it. Practice it until it feels natural. Being prepared when you pick up that phone will not only make you sound professional and in control, which will help you convey a positive telephone image, but it will also give you confidence and make the task of phoning for appointments that much easier.

2. *Be organized.* Remember, prospecting is an ongoing process, something which you must do regularly. Telephoning for appointments must become a regular part of your activity system and must be accomplished in an organized, efficient manner. You can do this in several ways.

   First, have a regular time and a regular place to make your calls. Some salespeople block out an hour or two each day. Others devote an entire day each week to calling. Work out a reasonable schedule, and then stick to it. Set goals. If you say you will call for appointments between 8:00 and 11:00 this morning or until you get ten appointments, whichever comes first, make sure you do not change your mind at 10:00 and go out for an early lunch. At the same time, reward yourself for little victories. Every time you get an appointment, take a stretch break and a quick amble about the office. However, avoid getting involved in water cooler office chatter; let your break last no more than a minute or two to keep your blood flowing.

Second, when you sit down to begin making those calls, be sure you have everything you need right there in front of you. This will include such things as:

- The entire list of prospects or prospect cards, complete with qualifying data and *phone numbers.* (Track down missing phone numbers in advance, not when calling for appointments.)

- Your appointment book or electronic device to record appointment times.

- A copy of your own telephone talk, with answers to objections.

- A "chit" sheet or computer program to record the outcome of each call, which you will transfer to your daily or weekly records, enabling you to keep a running table of your prospects-to-appointments ratio.

- A pad and pen or pencil for recording miscellaneous information.

- Your computer address book or a telephone directory (1) in case you have a wrong number and (2) to fill in with cold calls in the unfortunate event that you run out of prospects before obtaining the number of appointments you need.

By the way, if at all possible, organize names by how "hot" they appear to be as prospects. Call two or three weak prospects to help you warm up, then, once you're in swing, switch over to your best prospects. Save the remainder of the "least likelies" for last.

3. *Be enthusiastic.* Once the prospect answers the phone, you have less than 60 seconds to motivate him or her to grant you an appointment. And just because the prospect cannot see you, don't think that your attitude and your mood cannot be sensed. They can. Even — in fact, especially — if you have struck out with the last nine calls and obtained no appointments, you must pick up the phone believing, knowing, expecting to get an appointment on call number ten. How would you feel if you knew that the very next call you made would lead to the biggest single sale in the history of your company? Approach every call as if you expect that to happen. This enthusiasm will be directly reflected in your tone, in your attitude . . . and in your number of appointments.

4. *Develop a phone voice.* As part of your telephone personality, your voice is the key trait by which your prospects will judge you. Concentrate on developing a voice which is pleasant yet authoritative. It is not necessary for you to go to broadcast school to develop that clear, crisp, 11:00 news style. But here are a few tips which might help:

   • Learn to vary the level of your voice. Lower the volume, modulate the tone and put feeling into your words.

   • Slow down. People tend to speak more quickly when they feel they are under pressure. That tension is conveyed to prospects. Learn to reduce your rate of speech. You will sound more natural and relaxed.

- Act as if the prospect is in the room with you. Sit up in the chair and smile (yes, actually smile).

Dealing with Caller ID:

Most phones today have caller ID, which allows individuals to screen incoming calls. In this case, always leave a message that lets the prospect know who you are and why you are calling.

For example: *"(Name), I was referred to you by Tammy Smith, and I'm following up to make sure you received the email/letter I sent the other day about my products/services. If you could get back to me at (phone number), I would appreciate it very much. Thank you."*

You will likely want to follow up again by phone in about three days, and then again a week after that. By that time, if you have not made direct contact, it's time to quit. You cannot afford to waste time on non-prospects.

---

5. *Be brief.* Assume your prospect is a busy person. Immediately identify who you are and state the purpose of the call. Do not chat about the weather or last night's ball game or open with a sideshow come-on like, "Mr. Jones, how would you like an opportunity to buy the greatest invention since the wheel?" Keep the conversation short and to the point. Also, be sure not to slip into your sales presentation. Your objective is to get an appointment, not close the deal over the phone. While there is no hard-and-fast rule about how long, the call should last, try to keep it under four minutes.

6. *Be businesslike.* This is a business call. Treat it as such. Even if the prospect becomes argumentative, remain cool, calm, and in control. Banging down the receiver or insisting on winning an argument (even if you lose the prospect) are the kinds of things which can come

back to haunt you. So, promote a solid, businesslike posture with each call. It will help you in the long run.

7. *Sell only the appointment.* More appointments are lost because the salesperson became sidetracked and got embroiled in a lengthy discussion about the merits of the product or service over the phone. Your call has one and only one objective: *to secure an appointment with the prospect.* If the prospect wants to discuss your product or service over the phone, you may respond by saying something like, "I'd like to tell you more about my product, but frankly, it is difficult to do it justice over the phone. That's why I'd like to get together in person. Shall we say 11:30 on Tuesday? Or would 10:00 on Friday be better for you?"

8. *Ask for the appointment.* Strange as it may sound, some salespeople call up and chat, mention getting together, and never really ask for the appointment. So ask! Come right out and suggest getting together at a certain time on a certain day. The worst the prospect can say is "no." In that case, be prepared to…

9. *Ask again.* Most prospects will fire off an objection or two: "I'm sorry, but I'm awfully busy." "I'm really not interested, thank you." "Look, it's been a tough year and even if I wanted to, I don't have the cash." While you should not be rude, at the same time do not be afraid to be persistent. One experienced sales veteran explained his philosophy on calling for appointments this way:

> *Never hang up that phone until one of three possible things has happened; (1) you get the appointment; (2) you have asked for the appointment at least three times; or (3) the prospect hangs up on you.*

10. *Always end on a positive note.* Whatever the outcome of the conversation, end the call in a friendly, positive manner. If the

prospect refuses an appointment, try to leave the door open for another call at a later date. Many sales professionals have found that the second contact six months later very often pays off in an appointment.

Respect the Do-Not-Call Laws:
There are federal and state laws that restrict phone calls from salespeople. The fines can be extremely high. Be sure to check with a sales manager about the rules in your state and be sure not to cold-call anyone on the restricted list.

The Components of the Call

The call for an appointment may take no more than two or three minutes. However, a great many things transpire in that short time. Ideally, the seeds for a long-term relationship are sown with this call. So, let's take a careful look at what exactly is involved.

1. *The Introduction.* The purpose is to identify the prospect so you are sure you have the right person on the line; to identify yourself and your company; and to make sure your prospect has the time to talk to you. An effective introduction can be as simple as:

    "Hello, Mr. Newman? This is Bill Bradley with Ampersand Graphics. Do you have a moment?"

If the prospect hesitates or says, "It all depends on what you want," move immediately to the next component of the call. If he or she answers, "no," just say, "Thank you, that's fine. When would be a more convenient time to call?"

2. *The Approach.* The approach establishes the reason for the call and identifies any common ground between the prospect and yourself. If the prospect is a referral, mention the referrer's name. Instantly, you may be elevated from the status of a faceless stranger to that of the friend of a friend or associate. You may actually able to feel the change in attitude as the prospect's tone of voice shifts from being suspiciously cautious to more open and receptive. If you sent a pre-approach letter, ask if he or she received it. (The answer can be yes or no; either way, proceed.) Also at this time, indicate the nature of your service or product.

> *"I've done work with Jack Wells over at United Flex and he mentioned that our new mega-processor might be as beneficial to you as it was for him. 'That's why I'm calling. I'd like to get together at a convenient time to discuss that and possibly some other ideas you may find valuable."*

3. *The Close.* Phoning for an appointment is a kind of sale unto itself: you are selling the appointment. This is where you *ask* for the appointment. Be as specific as possible. Do not ask, "Can we get together sometime?" That is begging for rejection. Instead, either recommend a choice of two alternate times:

> *"Will it be possible to get together at 3:30 on Tuesday, or would 11:00 Friday be better?"*

or select a day and let the prospect pick a convenient time:

> *"Is there a convenient time next week we can get*

together for about 30 minutes? Say, on Wednesday?"

Note that you are employing *assumed consent* in asking for the appointment. The question is not, *"Can we get together?"* It is *"When can we get together?"* This approach assumes the prospect's consent to the appointment.

4.   *The Confirmation.* Once you have the appointment, confirm the time and location of the meeting, and end the call.

"Your office is located at 7914 Palmer Street, is that right?"

(Prospect response)

"Very good, Mr. Newman. I'll be looking forward to seeing you at your office on Wednesday, the 9th, at 9:00 a.m. Thank you and good-bye."

If the Prospect Raises Objections

Remember what we said earlier: prospects may not climb all over themselves to see you. They are busy people and, since they may not know you if they fell over you, they have no reason to welcome you with open arms. Regardless of how charming, disarming and professional you are, you are going to get objections.

Expect them . . . but do not accept them! The rule of thumb is to hang in through at least three objections. Following are several "universal" answers to objections. They will help you determine if the objection is real or just an evasion. Remember, if the prospect really does not have the time or interest to grant you an appointment, you will not get one. But it would be a shame to walk away from an appointment simply because the prospect was not *completely sure* he or she was in the market for your service or product.

While it is not recommended that you be pushy, at the same time do not be afraid to be persistent. When a prospect says: "Look, I'm not interested"; or "Thanks, but I already use somebody else"; or "Listen, I really don't have the time"; or "It's been a bad year; I couldn't buy any if I wanted to," try one of the following responses, then move right into the close:

"Fine, Mr. _____, I can appreciate that. In fact that's why I called. I know you may not be in the market right now. And even if you were, well, you don't know me. That's why I'd like to drop by to introduce myself and tell you a little about my product/my service. You'll be under no obligation. Would Wednesday at 9:30 be convenient?

or

"I understand, Miss _____. However, I would like the opportunity to drop by and introduce myself. So, let me make a suggestion. If you give me 15 minutes out of your day so that I can tell you a little about my product/my service, you'll be under no obligation. And there won't be a second appointment unless you desire it. Fair enough?"

or

"I realize that this may not be the best time to get together. However, sometime when I'm in your area I would like to drop by and introduce myself. Or call you again in the future. Do you have any objections to that?"

The above tracks are just samples. Take them as a starting point — adapt them, mold them to your own products and style of selling. And have them ready. You may even want to write them out and keep them in front of you while you are calling.

In this chapter, you learned how to turn a prospect into an appointment. In Chapter Six, we will discuss the things you should know about your prospect, your products, and yourself before going into that appointment, as well as what you should do in that first crucial face-to-face meeting.

Chapter Six

Preparing for the Interview:
The Mind of the Prospect

When you begin the interview, when you walk in the door, something starts to happen. People who very possibly were complete strangers before spend ten, 20 or 30 minutes together in a fairly intense exchange of information, ranging from verbally and electronically (such as PowerPoint presentations) expressed ideas and opinions to a wealth of nonverbal messages communicating attitudes and feelings. By the end of the meeting, a relationship exists between the two people. They may have established a common ground of respect and a willingness to work together. Or they may emerge detesting each other and vowing never to see each other again. Nonetheless, a great deal has transpired during those few minutes. And since you want the results to be positive, you must approach each and every sales interview with a clear sense of what you wish to accomplish and how best you can accomplish it.

As a well-prepared sales professional, you should enter the sales interview fully armed with product knowledge and effective selling techniques. But that is only part of selling. There is yet another aspect of preparing for the interview, one that is all too often ignored or overlooked. Before meeting your prospect face-to-face, it's imperative that you have at least a general understanding of what he or she is thinking and how he or she is going to react to you and your ideas.

Most prospects will not enter that first meeting ready to buy. Even if they acknowledge a need, they may not be sure what product best fills that need, or that they will buy it today or that they will buy it from you.

So let's examine the mind of the prospect. Let's try to pinpoint what he or she is thinking as you extend your hand and introduce yourself. Earlier, I said that a degree in psychology is not a prerequisite for a successful career in selling. And I have no intention of changing that now. What I are going to do, however, is provide you with some insight into typical reactions that you can expect at the beginning of that first face-to-face contact with a prospect.

Understanding Your Prospect

Why is it so important to understand how a prospect thinks? If you have ever played poker or chess or have been peacefully married for more than ten years, the answer is obvious. Take poker, for instance. In a poker game the cards in a player's hand alone do not determine the winner. The cards must be *played.* And the method of play of each player must be understood by the winning player. It is not uncommon for a player with a losing hand to bluff out one with a higher hand . . . if he knows how to read that player. For example, most players behave one way when the cards are mediocre, another way when they have a great hand and a third way when they are trying to bluff. Each player's play, within reason, is predictable.

Chess is similar. In chess, two people confront each other in a series of carefully planned maneuvers, each for the purpose of capturing the other's king. The victor is the player who has not only perfected his own playing skills, but who has also learned to anticipate his opponent's moves. He has learned through observation, intuition, and competing what his opponent is thinking and how he will react in most situations.

Marriage is most like the sales situation. In chess or poker, there is a winner and a loser, the victor and the vanquished. But a happy marriage requires that both sides benefit, both sides win. That is what makes it similar to a sales situation. Though there are many ingredients that make up a harmonious marriage, one of the most important is understanding how the other thinks. For example:

Jon has had one of those days. Of his four scheduled sales interviews, three did not buy and one was a no-show. To top things off, he had a flat tire and got grease all over his best suit while changing it. All he wants now is to retreat home for a nice dinner and a peaceful evening with Liz and the kids.

But as he walks into the house, chaos greets him. He learns that the washing machine backed up and flooded the basement, the dog dug up half the garden, and the delivery people failed to come. The look in Liz's eyes indicates that she is suffering from an advance case of cabin fever and is on the verge of blowing her top.

Jon could simply blunder in the door, aware only of his own needs and oblivious to all else. But because he is tuned into Liz, understands that look in her eyes, senses the tension stewing in her, he shifts his priorities, gets a babysitter for the kids, and takes Liz out for a quiet dinner, during which they both begin to recover from the day.

Jon understands both his wife and the value of win-win situations. If he had plowed through that front door, bemoaning his bad day, and demanded dinner, what would have followed would have been the icing on the cake — an evening of quarreling to top off a day of setbacks. Everyone would lose. Let's look at another example.

Bob sat at the table excitedly going over every feature of that sports car he wanted to get. It was a convertible, the right color, had a super CD and satellite sound system, and the price that was not too bad.

Mary listened patiently. Yes, she told herself, they could probably afford it. But it would put a strain on their budget. They also needed a new furnace for the house. Plus, with three children, a sports car just was not practical. Bob was one of the most levelheaded people she knew. But once in a while, he would get his heart set on something out of the blue ... . and that would be it. Mary knew that the worst thing she could do was to come right out and tell Bob what she was thinking. She would have to approach the subject cautiously, helping Bob see that the idea was not a good one at this time.

"Bob, you know the decision is yours," she began. "You said that it would cost an additional $600 a month."

Mary began by asking the right questions. It was not long before Bob himself would have second thoughts about the advisability of the purchase. But it was only by asking the right questions that Mary was able to help Bob arrive at the best decision for all. She was able to do this because she knew Bob. She knew that he was levelheaded and would see things more clearly when he began figuring the dollars and cents of the situation.

Most of all, she knew that to attack or ridicule his decision would have been the worst thing she could have done. Not only would it have caused a fight, but it also would have polarized them into opposing camps. After that, whatever the outcome, whether Bob bought the car or not, both of them would have been miserable. Brinkmanship and confrontation politics do not work in marriage or sales. And just as Jon in the previous example had the sense to put his own needs on the back burner and provide Liz with what she needed most, just as Mary was able to motivate Bob to make the decision which was best for everyone concerned; you too must approach selling with that same frame of mind and interest in working with prospects to establish a mutually beneficial relationship.

Why is it important to understand your prospects? Because it will help you answer their questions before they arise, understand their needs, anticipate their objections, and gear your presentation to motivate them to buy.

You have to know what makes them tick, what motivates them, what affects them. Some sales professionals believe that selling is 98% people knowledge, and 2% product knowledge. While I would not go that far, it is true that the more you know about your prospects — their attitudes, the way they do business, how they think and act — the more successful you will be.

There is only one thing wrong with the application of this theory to sales. You do not know these individuals closely, if at all. If you play poker with the same group long enough, you begin to learn the characteristics of each player. You know that George's ears get red when he has a good hand, that Maynard fidgets in his chair when he bluffs, that Keith raises his eyebrows and scans the faces of the other players when he is sure he is the winner. The same thing can happen in a chess game between old friends who have played together for years. They learn how each other thinks after a while, how one will react to the other's moves. And as for marriage, it is not uncommon, given enough years together, for couples to just about know each other's thoughts.

You do not have that luxury of time to get to know your prospect. You may be meeting a complete stranger for the first time. And in the ten minutes or so that follow, you have to establish a relationship and be well on the road to completing a sale. You do not know this person and certainly do not have the time to acquire a detailed knowledge of his or her personal likes or dislikes. It is believed that a sale takes place when — and only when — there is a meeting of the minds, when the buyer and the seller come to agreement. But how can you reach a meeting of the minds when you do not even know what your prospect is thinking? The answer is that you *do* know what he or she is thinking. Or at least you know what others have thought and done in similar situations.

I am talking about being aware of the averages, about studying the norms. Once again, we are not looking for stereotypes. Your prospects are individuals. However, people in general tend to react in predictable ways in response to certain situations.

In the sales interview, most prospects can be expected to react in a relatively predictable manner throughout, beginning with that introductory handshake. For instance, when you first meet a prospect, which kind of reaction can you expect? He or she will probably shake your hand, but remain cool, aloof, cautious. Whether the prospect initiated the appointment or it came about as the result of your efforts, he or she is going to spend the first few minutes sizing you up, judging you by the firmness of your handshake, the style of your clothes, the expression on your face, the shine on your shoes. The prospect is also wondering what you will say and do. Are you a high- pressure arm twister? A slick, fast talker? The prospect will be skeptical. And why not? Don't you react this way when you're on the buying side in a sales situation? The burden of proof is on the seller. Prospects have to be shown, at every step, that you are not wasting their time, that you really do have something of value to discuss with them. Because, just as you know nothing about them personally, they know even less about you. So, depending on the individual, a prospect may begin the interview with one or more of the following thoughts running through his or her mind:

"I know exactly how to get rid of this salesperson ... and quick!"

Many prospects have developed a highly effective un-sales talk designed to dispatch the salesperson in short order. It may start off as, "No, I'm only browsing" or "I'm pleased with my present carrier." And it can heat up to, "I'd rather look around myself" or "Look, I personally hate this stuff and the people who sell it."

"I see no profit in giving this person my time."

These prospects want to choose for themselves how they spend their time, which they consider to be highly valuable ... and rightly so. They will let you know when and if they are ready to buy. Then all you will be expected to do is take the order. They do not want to have their time wasted and are afraid you are going to do just that.

"Here comes the sales pressure, and I don't intend to put up with it."

Some prospects feel that you are intruding into their territory, invading their privacy. As a result they tense up, become defensive. Since they do not know your intentions, they are going to gird for war and be prepared for the worst. Unfortunately, these prospects view you as an adversary and fear that there will be attempts on your part to manipulate them.

"I'm not going to buy anything. Period!"

Based on the same fear of sales pressure as in the previous thought, prospects may simply set their minds firmly on the word "no" and shut down the mental process. This kind of thinking can be summarized with the statement, "Don't bother me with the facts. I know what I plan to do."

"I can't afford it."

Sometimes this is true. At other times, it is a matter of perception and priorities. You can never afford what you do not think is important or valuable enough to own. On the other hand, you probably know people who wear cardboard to cover the holes in their shoes, yet vacation two weeks out of each year in the Virgin Islands.

Back in the late 1950's and early 1960's, when color television was coming into its own, a set could cost as much as $1,000. If you think that is a lot of money today, remember that those were pre-inflation dollars when the average household income was under $10,000. So, let's say the equivalent is close to $5,000 today. A lot of money. But amazingly enough, it was not the rich who made color television a success, but people in the lower-middle and upper-lower income classes, the people who had saved up to buy new shoes for their children each September and saw steak as a luxury.

Or there are the young couples who struggle to make their car and rent payments, but who have state-of-the-art music and home entertainment systems in their apartments, along with every new-n-improved electronic gizmo and video game that comes out. They sell – and are bought -- because of perceived need. Because of priorities. It is true that people sometimes flat out cannot afford a certain product. However, be aware that when a prospect may be thinking (or, if you are fortunate, comes right out and says) "I can't afford it," this does not necessarily close the door on a possible sale. On the contrary, it simply means that it is your job to help establish the need in their minds.

"I don't know this salesperson. Why should I do business with him/her?"

And this final point is a good one. Nobody likes to deal with a stranger. What you must do is make yourself something more than a stranger, and do it quickly.

Breaking the Barrier

The above are examples of what may be running through a prospect's mind as you meet. It may seem as though the odds are stacked pretty heavily against you, that you may remain forever outside in the cold, tapping on the window. Fortunately, this need not be the case. In fact, there are a number of rather simple yet highly effective ways for you to break down that barrier and gain access to the inside.

First and foremost, as we have said before, use good common sense. If a prospect appears defensive or uneasy, do not plunge blindly ahead, ignoring all the danger signals. Make sure you ease the "relationship tension" between you and the prospect before proceeding. To do this you must *sell yourself* before you can ever sell a product.

A second way to overcome the prospect's concerns and anxiety and open the door to a friendly, effective selling interview is simply to treat your prospect with courtesy. It does go a long way. Apply the Golden Rule: "Treat others as you would have them treat you." Take that Golden Rule and make it law. It is amazing how some salespeople, in the name of business, would subject other people to the most annoying, intimidating practices. However, if they would only treat these same prospects with respect — as dignified, sensitive, intelligent human beings, instead of "marks" in a con job to be manipulated into buying — they would be taking a major step forward on the road to their own success.

You are not training to be a hit-and-run artist, but a sales professional. And you should at the same time never be too polite to ask for that sale (politeness has nothing to do with it). However, you must have enough faith in yourself and your product to offer your product, make your best presentation, and be willing to accept a possible "no." It is possible to ram through a sale virtually by intimidating the prospect. But the salesperson who resorts to such selling-by-intimidation tactics is indulging in short-sightedness and is really cutting his or her own throat.

Another way to break down that initial resistance — and to earn the prospect's respect throughout the interview — is to learn to listen and observe. Too many times salespeople are so eager to talk about their product that they talk themselves out of sales. The prospect may be screaming out one need while the salesperson blithely tries to meet another, possibly nonexistent, need. Note the following conversation:

Salesperson: "We have this terrific new term life insurance policy. And we can set you up with the amount you need for about $200 a year."

Prospect: "I've always been partial to permanent life coverage. It builds cash values and eventually pays for itself."

Salesperson: "What you might want to do is buy this term policy and then we can look at some other investment options, such as mutual funds."

The salesperson was not listening. He was more interested in what he wanted to sell than in what the prospect wanted to buy.

And of course, there is the classic scene where the customer walks into a store knowing exactly what he wants:

Customer: "I'd like to see a pair of those black wing-tip shoes like the ones I saw in the window."

Salesperson: "Certainly, we have those in brown also."

Customer: "I'd like them in black, please."

Salesperson: "We also have loafers. Beautiful new designs from Italy. Let me show you a pair."

It may seem silly when you read it, but it happens. Every day salespeople lose sales because they were not paying attention. Some of the best advice you can receive on the subject is: *know when to shut up. Know when to listen.*

The Correct Sales Posture

For most sales professionals, the question, "How should I approach a prospect?" also entails deciding what kind of attitude or demeanor or behavior would best be suited for the sale and would most enhance the relationship with the prospect. Now again, while every prospect is an individual and every selling situation is unique, a few general observations can still be made.

Many salespeople believe that the more aggressive they are, the better they can present their case and make the sale. Still others, fearful of alienating the prospect, tend to adopt a passive approach. Neither one is the correct sales posture. The aggressive salesperson, because of his or her domineering attitude, often cuts off communication at the outset of the interview, leaving the prospect either openly or secretly humiliated and angry. If, by chance, this salesperson bullies his or her way into closing the sale, it will remain on the books only a short time, and there is little likelihood of any repeat appointments or sales opportunities with the same prospect. At the opposite end of the spectrum, a passive approach, characterized by indirectness, self-denial and inhibition, more often than not leaves the seller feeling hurt, anxious and angry with him or herself. The prospect is apt to experience irritation, pity and disgust — feelings that certainly are not conducive to a successful selling environment.

Both aggressive and passive salespeople deny themselves the all-important win-win situation. Somewhere in between these two extremes lies the optimum, and that is, *assertive* behavior, which is characterized by direct, expressive communications. The assertive salesperson treats his or her prospects as equals, making them feel respected and valued, feelings they in turn attach to the salesperson. The assertive salesperson, instead of worrying what the prospect (or manager, or associate or spouse) may think or do, concentrates instead on his or her own thoughts and actions and follows them with conviction because he or she knows they are right and believes in them. The assertive salesperson is able to enter the interview with confidence and, whether a sale is made or not, leave it with self-respect.

The initial face-to-face encounter with a prospect is extremely important and the salesperson's behavior and attitude — much more so than the prospect's — are key ingredients as to how well or how poorly that encounter will go. This is where the assertive salesperson shines. He or she understands that at this early stage in the selling process, the prospect may be feeling apprehensive or uncertain about the seller's interest, competence or what will be asked of him or her. The assertive seller, therefore, seeks to put the prospect at ease while establishing a businesslike posture: non-intrusive and non-threatening, yet attentive and alert. In such a way, the sales –professional effectively controls the situation and enhances the probability of a successful outcome to the sale.

Appearances Count

Another aspect of professionalism and another way to impress — or distress — your prospect is your appearance. Whether we like to admit it or not, we all tend to judge — and are in turn judged — by appearances. Dress appropriately. If your prospects wear three-piece suits, do the same. At the minimum, wear a sports coat and tie, regardless of what they wear. And make sure that everything is neat and clean, and you are well-groomed: shoes shined, hands spotless, hair impeccable. In short, dress tastefully and look respectable. You will be amazed at the impression this will make.

Is a suit always appropriate? That's a tough call, especially in these days of "business casual" dress. On one hand, the two-piece suit for men and the dark colored pantsuit for women always are appropriate, if only because it tells the prospect that you are a professional. (What would you think if a doctor came to the clinic wearing jeans and ratty t-shirt?) On the other hand, dress is more casual than it was 20 or 30 years ago. At the very least, men should wear a dress shirt and usually a tie and sports coat. Women have a wider range of acceptable dress, but they should lean to the more serious side.

If you doubt that people are judged by their appearances, try this little experiment. Get up next Saturday and put on the raggediest shirt and pair of pants you have (no designer jeans). Men, do not shave. Women, skip the makeup. Do not comb your hair. Then spend an hour or so working in the garden. Finally, without cleaning up, go down to the nearest Lexus dealership and walk into the showroom. You may be totally ignored. You may get some curious, passing interest. But do not expect a test drive. On Monday, return to the same dealership. This time, however, be dressed in your best business attire. Note the difference in the way you are perceived and treated by the salespeople on the floor. Appearance does make a difference. See for yourself.

Common sense, courtesy, the ability to listen and observe, along with your professional appearance and assertive manner will help you bridge the distance between your prospects and you. However, none of this replaces the need to *be prepared,* the necessity of knowing your products and services and being able to present them in a stimulating, motivating and intelligent manner. This is the subject of our next chapter.

Chapter Seven

The Organized Sales Presentation

You've made it. The hours of planning, preparing, organizing and prospecting have paid off, and now you're sitting in front of a prospect. You're ready to make your presentation, close the sale and walk out the door with a signed order or application in hand. But are you really ready? Are you really prepared? This step of the sales cycle is critical and you can't afford to make a mistake.

When you sit down with a prospect for the first time, in every sense of the phrase — THIS IS IT! This is your purpose as a sales professional: placing yourself in a situation that can lead to a sale. This is your moment of glory, your time in the spotlight. It is not the time to meander in the door and decide to play it by ear, to ad-lib as you go along. You must enter prepared; you must enter ready to sell. Remember our definition of selling from Chapter One:

**SELLING IS THE ACTIVE PROCESS
OF PRESENTING INFORMATION IN SUCH A MANNER
THAT IT MOTIVATES AND GUIDES
THE OTHER PARTY
TO TAKE A SPECIFIED ACTION.**

Effective selling is the "active process of presenting information." And that is the theme of this chapter: to discus how best you can present your information, how most effectively you can make your case to your prospect. This can be done through the *organized sales presentation*.

The organized sales presentation is a process, a series of interrelated steps, whereby you:

1. Sell yourself

2. Sell the need/problem

3. Sell the solution

4. Sell the sale

5. Obtain referrals

These five steps have been described in many ways by many people. There is nothing new about them. They have been around for a while, and that is because they work and they have proven to be effective. Let's take a look at each of these steps.

Step One: Selling Yourself

This is also known as the approach or introduction. Simply enough, it takes place at the opening of the interview, during which you introduce yourself and begin establishing the basis for a long-term relationship. Specifically, the objective is to establish rapport, and a common ground. Think for a moment just how important this is. When you buy something, why do you shop where you do? Of course, price and quality are factors. However, is not your own comfort level also important? People do not shop where they do not feel at home, where they are made to feel awkward, uncomfortable, or unwelcome. On the other hand, people enjoy doing business where they feel they are welcome, where they feel they have friends.

I have lunch about twice a week in a particular restaurant in my hometown. When I enter, I am always greeted by name by either the owner or an employee. I immediately feel welcome, to the point that I sometimes say, "Janelle, what do I want for lunch today?" There are other restaurants in town. There is nothing really all that special about this one, except that I have been made to feel at home there. Whether I'm by myself, or with a business associate or friend, I always receive the same warm, friendly service. That is why I eat there regularly.

In your own sales efforts, simply remember that before you can sell a product, you must first sell yourself. Get to know the prospect, and give him or her a chance to get to know you. Sometimes two people meet and they "click." Instant rapport. They like each other. Most of the time, however, a relationship has to be built. Like anything else in sales, it does not just happen. It has to be *made* to happen.

Depending on the type of product or service you sell, you may be able to do this in a single meeting, completing the entire sales process from intro to conclusion in an hour or so. Or you may need to cultivate relationships over time. I have clients I have known for years. I also have prospects I have known for a long time, too, but they are not yet clients. It may happen. It may not. But every time we talk or email, we strengthen that personal relationship just a little bit more.

But now let's look at the first time you meet a new prospect face to face. In the previous chapter, you learned about what the prospect may be thinking as he or she meets you, and you learned ways to make that first impression as positive as possible.

Specifically, however, how do you make that happen? First, logically enough, identify yourself. At the same time, find out how much the prospect already knows about you. This can be a very natural way to begin the conversation, especially if the prospect is a referral:

"Mr. Blackburn, my name is Alex Grant. It's a pleasure to finally meet you in

person. Mary Wilson (the referrer) has told me a little about you. But tell me, has Mary told you anything about me?"

This not only establishes the name of the referrer as the first thread of commonality between you and the prospect, but it gives you the opportunity to (1) find out exactly what the prospect has learned about you from the referrer; (2) clear up any misinformation he or she may have received; and (3) provide the prospect with a detailed (but brief) background on who you are and why he or she should talk to you.

Here is one example of how an estate planning professional I knew years ago would introduce himself at the start of the appointment.

What He'd Say	Why He'd Say It
"Has (referrer) told you any- thing about the work that I do? Well, before I get into that I'd like to tell a little about myself so I'm not a complete stranger to you.	Determines how much the prospect knows about him and his service
"I've been doing this work for about 20 years. I have an undergraduate degree in econo- mics and finance, and I have taught these subjects at the university level.	Briefly states his credentials to do the work, creating credibility.
"I am not an accountant and I am not an attorney; however, I do work in such areas as estate planning and tax law. I am not interested in replacing your at- torney or accountant . . . but rather	Anticipates possible questions concerning duplicating work of other professionals

my work will supplement what they do.	
"I've chosen to work with people like yourself because I've found there are far more tax-saving and financial planning opportunities in working with business owners (or professionals, or company executives, etc.). And if I can't save you taxes and other estate costs, I won't propose to do the work for you because I'm not interested in wasting your time."	States potential benefits of service.

Your introduction is your opening salvo. It sets the tone and mood for what follows. If it is effective, it may make the sale. If it rolls over, whines and plays dead, nothing you say or do that follows may pull the sale out of the fire. That is why it is so important to give the introduction your best shot.

In fact, it is strongly recommended that you put down this book before going on to Step Two and create a one- or two-minute introduction of your own. This is also known as your "elevator talk," a brief summary of who you are and what you do. (The original concept was to create a talk designed to stimulate interest in your or your services that could be delivered on a brief elevator ride with a potential prospect.)

My 30-second Elevator Talk

Your elevator talk will change and evolve over time and for different situations. I have several versions. Here is the one-floor elevator talk:

I'm John Ingrisano. I have been a sales trainer and marketing strategist for 30 years. I work with clients as big as Ameriprise Financial, New York Life and Resort Condominiums International (RCI), as well as small businesses around the region.

I'm also a business columnist and have been described as "The Voice of the Freestyle Entrepreneur." My role is to help my clients survive, thrive and prosper.

Make sure your elevator talk is relevant and to the point, emphasizing any appropriate experience and accomplishments on your part, the reputation of your company and the purpose of your visit.

Once you have the introduction the way you like it, the next step is to *learn it*. Know it so well that it flows easily, smoothly and without effort. Then use it with each and every sales interview, as well as every time a potential prospect asks, "What do you do?"

Step Two: Selling the Need/Problem

Few people are going to buy anything unless they perceive a need for it. There are folks who will buy anything if they think it is a real bargain. These are the ones with attics and garages stuffed full of crates of size 12 army boots, half-worn retread tires, cases of Tabasco sauce, and boxes of ties — bought at five cents on the dollar — that even Flippo the Clown would be too embarrassed to wear. These people exist. But they are not the norm.

Most people and businesses spend their money cautiously. They may not squeeze every dime they spend, but they will hug them a bit before letting go. They may want to own a new Mercedes, but can also live with the decision to keep that reliable six-year-old Chevrolet wagon through one more season. They may want to stay at the Ritz while traveling, but have no objection to the Budget Inn. They may want the latest top-of-the-line, state-of-the-art, whiz-bang computer for their company, but they realize they may not grow into it for several years and might be better advised to put the cash they would be saving into inventory expansion. In other words, most people do not throw their money around, and you had better not walk through the door and expect them to start stuffing it into your pockets.

Once again, people will only buy your product if they have a need for it. More specifically, they will only buy it if they *believe* they have a need for it. This can be interpreted in two ways:

1. They have a genuine need and — either through their own self-awareness or the efforts of a sales professional — are aware of that need. (Remember, it is quite possible for your prospect to be staring in the face of an obvious need for your product and yet be oblivious to that need).

2. They have a *perceived* need (more of a *want* than a need). Never discount a perceived need; it is just as real as a genuine need.

An example of the first type, a genuine need, might be the need for life insurance by a person with a spouse, five children, a high income, and little or no present coverage. The need here is alarmingly real. A perceived need is a bit different. It might include yearning for the sunny Caribbean while slogging through snowdrifts in Minneapolis, or wanting to buy that dream house on a lake while the present one is more than adequate. The point to remember is that, whether genuine or perceived, a need is as real as the prospect believes it to be.

For the sake of teaching you how to sell, let's assume that the prospect does not understand that there is a need or problem that your product can satisfy; in other words, the need is not apparent. The prospect does not readily see how your product will help cut costs or reduce overhead or provide for his family after his death or perhaps simply make his life a little easier. The prospect has to be convinced. The need has to be identified and then sold to the prospect. How? Through a two-step process:

Step One: Data Collection. You cannot even attempt to identify any need until you have the facts. You need pertinent information about the prospect and his or her situation. Nobody expects you to be a Houdini. You cannot look into a crystal ball and say, "You are troubled about your future. You are worried about what will happen to your business after you retire." You cannot do that. Nobody expects you to. And you will get into trouble if you try.

What do we mean by data collection? Well, it depends upon what you are selling, the method by which you are selling it, and what you may already know about your prospective buyer. If you are selling automobiles, data collection may consist of determining your customer's price range, the type of model in which he or she is interested – SUV, hybrid, sports car -- a range of features, the age and make of a possible trade-in, and so on. You probably will not even take notes.

On the other hand, if you are in insurance sales and meeting with a young family, you will need the following types of information: marital status, number of children and their ages, income of both husband and wife, type and amount of existing coverage, etc. You may gather this information on a legal pad or you may wish to design a short fact-finding form if your company does not already provide one. At the far end of the spectrum, such as estate planning and financial planning, data collection may require several hours and the forms can run from three or four pages to as many as 30 or so.

But forms alone may not provide you with all the data you require. As we have said, be observant, pay attention, use common sense. Attitudes are crucial. The important thing to remember is that the data you collect must be relevant. It must help you understand the needs of your prospect better so that you can provide the product or service which best suits those needs.

Step two: Identification of Needs. From the data you collect, you must then identify one or more needs and make sure that you and your prospective buyer agree that they are, in fact, needs that he or she perceives as such. This is where selling the need comes in. Do not underestimate the importance of this step. Without total agreement and understanding on the prospect's part here, the rest of the sales presentation will collapse. You cannot motivate prospects to solve problems that they do not recognize as problems.

My father was a successful physician. At one point I recommended that he consider some estate planning work and introduced him to a financial advisor. My father was a top-drawer medical man, but as is often the case with such professionals, he had failed to make even the most rudimentary plans for the care of his family and the distribution of his estate at his death. During a brief fact-finding session, the advisor learned that most of my father's assets were in relatively non-liquid assets. Also, while his estate was worth just under a million dollars, his total life insurance coverage was only about $20,000, which he thought was quite sufficient.

My father cared a great deal about his family, but he did not understand that the present casual arrangement of his estate plan would cause my mother great hardship. He did not fully understand that assets might have to be sold, possibly at bargain prices, to settle his estate when he died, and that my mother would be left with no income. As far as he was concerned, he had no problem. It was up to the advisor to educate him, to make him understand what could happen to his the family if he died with the way things were presently arranged. That was a necessary prerequisite before the advisor could even suggest the purchase of life insurance.

Remember that until (and unless) prospective buyers can be shown that they have a problem or a need, they will see no reason to implement a solution, and there will be no sale.

Once you have identified a need, how do you communicate it to a prospect? Sometimes you can take a rather direct approach:

"Bill, it is obvious to me that you are spending a disproportionate amount of your costs on marketing in relation to the results you are seeing. Many of my other clients have ratios that look twice as good."

or

"Tom, Social Security is designed only to provide a floor of protection, not serve as a complete retirement package. If you do not start socking away a portion of your current earnings starting right now, you may find yourself unable to afford to retire when you plan to."

or

"John, you have a problem. You are not getting a good return on this for what you are putting into it. See what I mean?"

This approach may work when the needs are obvious. To make it work, here is how to make the prospect aware of the need:

1. Summarize pertinent data that helped you arrive at the conclusion that there is a need. Depending upon the nature of the sale, this may require as long as an hour or two or as short as 30 seconds.

2. Obtain agreement at each step of the summary, using such phrases as, "Don't you agree?" or "Does this sound about right?" This provides you with a constant source of feedback and helps the prospect recognize and commit to his or her own situation. If the prospect agrees that you are on target with each of, say, five separate problem areas, there is an excellent chance he or she will agree to and understand what you are saying in summary regarding the *entire* problem.

3. Summarize the problem or need as clearly and as succinctly as possible.

A highly effective approach to carrying out these three steps is to move from the general to the specific. Psychologically, most people do not like to be told they are not already doing something in the best possible manner. They do not like to hear such things as:

- *"If you died tomorrow, your children probably wouldn't be able to afford to go to college."*

- *"Your present marketing system is the most inefficient possible."*

- *"I'm not surprised you have a problem. You bought Acme's product."*

- *"This may sound good now. But ten years down the road, you '11 realize you made a mistake. And by then, it will be too late to do anything about it."*

Now while there's something to be said for taking the bull by the horns, there's also a simple matter of tact. When identifying a need or problem to your prospects, you must be very careful not to offend them or put them on the defensive. You have just spent time during the approach/ introduction attempting to build rapport and lay the groundwork for a mutually beneficial buyer-seller relationship. If you then turn around and insult your prospects' intelligence, ability, or common sense -- either directly or by allusion -- you may very well destroy the tenuous beginnings of the relationship which you have worked so hard to establish.

Instead, put prospects in good company by using comparisons, by alluding to others who may have done things exactly the way they did. There is comfort in being part of a group. In school, we did not mind getting a low grade if everyone else received one as well. It is not so much that misery likes company as that we do not feel stupid if everyone else -- or at least people we respect -- makes the same error or does things the same way. This means you should help your prospects identify with a group that has the same problem.

For instance, instead of saying:

"If you died tomorrow, your children probably wouldn't be able to go to college," soften the blow by saying something like the following:

"When you and I went to school, it was possible to do so on a pay-as-you-go basis. I know when I went my father paid my tuition, partially from savings, partially *from current income and partially from 4% loans. I paid for my own room and board through part-time jobs during the school year and full-time jobs in the summer. How about you? (Prospect response) Then it was possible, what with the annual costs of a college education being so low. But college costs have skyrocketed since we went to school, running as high as tens of thousands of dollars a year for some schools."*

Or instead of saying:

"Your present marketing system is the most inefficient possible," open with a less threatening approach, such as:

"A number of companies about the size of yours started out using this same

system years ago. And it worked great for a long time. But many of these same companies are discovering that the marketing climate is changing. The cost of labor has skyrocketed. Why, even the cost of mailing a letter has gone up about 500% since you started doing business, right? The problem is that most of these companies are finding that they can no longer afford to do business that way."

You must obtain some sign of agreement from prospects at this point. Encourage them to talk about how *they* feel about what you are saying. Assume you are a car salesperson and your prospect has shown mild interest in a luxury automobile, but for practical reasons is considering a smaller, downsized car for reasons of economy. The conversation may go something like this:

YOU: "A number of people made the switch to down-sized cars recently, often to save gas. But I've heard a number of people complain that, while they gained in gas mileage, it was at the expense of comfort and performance. Do you know what I mean? How many miles a year do you drive? I know that when I take long trips, I want to arrive feeling refreshed, not cramped and sore."

PROSPECT: "You know, that's a good point. A friend of mine has one of those little ones. They can be cramped, and even then the mileage isn't all that great.

From that point on, half the battle is won. Once the prospect agrees to the general nature of the problem, the next step is to focus the problem closer to home, to bring it from the general to the specific. Here's another example:

"Do you realize that while almost everyone agrees that adequate amounts of life insurance are a necessity, most of the people who die during their working years have barely enough coverage to bury them, settle their estates and care for their surviving family members for a year or two? That's not just talk. It's true. It

*happens to people every day. That's why I want to talk with you. From what
you have told me, it seems that you have about $85,000 of life insurance
coverage between your individual policies and the coverage you receive through
work. If you died tonight, about $10,000 of that amount would go toward
burying you. If we ignore the cost of settling your estate, that would leave
$75,000 for Dorothy and your two children to get by on. How long do you think
that would last?"*

The objective is to take prospects -- who up to this point have been
something of disinterested bystanders listening to you talk about other
people's problems -- and transform them into active participants. The
problem must change from being someone else's to being his or hers. The
prospects must see that they have a problem in need of a solution, that they
have a need that is not being met. You must sell the need. You must *disturb*
prospects in the sense that they must be made to understand that there is a
situation that requires action.

Step Three: Selling the Solution

By this point, the prospect should be acutely aware that there is a problem,
a need that is currently unfulfilled. If you have done your job properly, the
prospect should also be acutely interested in what you have to say. You are
the person who has made him or her aware of a problem. And you are also
the person who can offer a solution to that problem. Now is the time for
you to share it with your prospect.

(In some instances, especially in more complex estate and financial
planning situations, the sales process involves at least two interviews. In
the first, data is collected and apparent problems are briefly summarized.
Then, before the actual presentation, there is a program development step
during which the sales professional reviews and analyzes the data and
develops a suitable plan or recommendations that should meet the
prospect's needs. Then in the second interview, key elements of the data

are briefly summarized, key problems or needs are identified, and the solution is presented.)

Perhaps you have helped a business owner realize that there is a problem with his present record keeping system, production facilities, marketing design, pension plan, office equipment, or whatever. He now knows that there is a problem, that something is not up to snuff. Perhaps you have helped a purchasing manager realize that her present supplier is too expensive or too slow or providing products that are no longer state-of-the-art quality. Perhaps you have helped a husband and wife realize that retirement is "only" 25 years away, or that if one of them died, the survivor and the children would be hard pressed to get by, let alone maintain their present comfortable standard of living.

In other words, your prospect is disturbed/worried/concerned about his or her present situation. In the accepted jargon of the professional salesperson, you have "disturbed the status quo." And that's good.

Now what do you do? Just as you made prospects aware of a problem or need, you must now guide them gently toward the solution. More than that, you must sell the solution. Just because people recognize a problem does not mean they will take the necessary action to correct it. The next step, therefore, is to sell prospects on the appropriateness of the solution you have to offer. No matter what you are selling, no matter what the need, there are several key points to keep clearly in mind as you present your solution:

1. *Take a problem/solution approach.* This is another way of saying you should take a logical, organized approach. The idea is never to let the solution become too far removed from the problem. Always make sure that the prospect understands that the only reason there must be a solution is because there is a very real problem or need.

2. *Keep it simple.* Do not build cathedrals when gas stations will do nicely. If someone were to write the annals of lost sales, a major chapter would surely deal with salespeople who over-engineered their presentations, throwing in every detail and fact, asking the prospect to follow along on what may be a logical, yet overly convoluted and complex presentation.

3. *Sell the sizzle.* When a person walks into a restaurant in search of a good steak dinner, he is not buying a 16-ounce lump of cold, raw meat. He is buying the way that meat tastes and the way it smells when it is properly cooked. He is, in fact, buying the "sizzle." It is the same with any kind of sale. Sell the sizzle, not the hunk of dead cow. Translated, this means you should concentrate on the *benefits* of your product, not just its features. For example...

> *A woman 65 years old entered the automobile showroom. "Will you please tell me about this car?" she asked the young salesman. "Yes, Ma'am, "he enthusiastically began. "It's got a two-barrel carburetor, catalytic converter, a 240 cubic inch engine, six-stack CD player and Ipod mount, and super-chrome package all standard. It's also available with poly-belted radials, our maxi-5-years-or-50, 000-miles body integrity package, which includes rust-proofing."*

> *The woman listened patiently to the presentation. When the salesman had finished, she spoke up. "Yes, I understand all that, "she lied, "but will it get me to my son's house without breaking down?"*

The woman in this case did not want a car. She wanted a reliable means of traveling to see her family. She did not care one bit about the features of the car. She was interested in the benefits the car would bring. Every day salespeople make the same mistake as that young car salesman in our example did. They forget that what the prospect really cares about and really wants to hear about is a clearer, big-screen picture, a comfortable ride, better taste, or security for their family.

Features are only what the product consists of. Benefits are what those features will do for the prospect. Money is an excellent example. Money in itself is worthless. You cannot eat it. It cannot be driven. It won't keep you warm in the winter. It does absolutely nothing in and of itself. But what are its benefits? Money can buy warmth and shelter from the elements. It can buy food for nourishment, health and growth. It can buy every creature comfort. It can buy benefits!

You must learn to translate the features of your products into benefits for the prospects. If you are an automobile salesperson, you are not selling just a car. You are selling transportation, lifestyle, status, comfort, status and, quite often now, economy. If you are selling refrigerators, you are not selling just a cold box that makes ice cubes. You are selling the convenience and economy of fresh food, along with (possibly) digitalized video screens and electronic controls. If you are selling office equipment, you are not selling just a copier or computer. You are selling cost efficiency, speed, and increased profits. And if you are selling life insurance or your services as a financial planner, you are not selling policies or stocks or bonds or real estate or even money. You are selling financial security, comfortable retirements, peace of mind, a sense of accomplishment. Learn to see your product in terms of its benefits, not just its features. Features mean nothing unless they benefit the buyer.

Step Four: Selling the Sale

Even though you have made your prospect completely aware of glaring needs, and even though you have made it crystal clear that your product or service will fill those needs like a hand fills a glove, and even though your prospect agrees 100% with everything you have to say, that does not mean you have the sale in the bag. People do not always do what they know they should. It is similar to telling an overweight person that he needs to diet, or that a two-pack-a-day smoker needs to quit. They both know what they *should* do. The problem is that neither has been properly motivated to *act* and to act *now*.

Let's go back once again to that simple definition of selling and look at another key element:

**SELLING IS THE ACTIVE PROCESS
OF PRESENTING INFORMATION IN SUCH A MANNER
THAT IT MOTIVATES AND GUIDES
THE OTHER PARTY
TO TAKE A SPECIFIED ACTION.**

A successful sales presentation "motivates and guides the other party to take a specified action." What happens if you drop the ball at this point, if you fail to close the sale? Then you have had a pleasant chat, an informational session and nothing more. The prospect may say, "I like it. It sounds like an excellent plan/idea/service. I should do something about it." But if he or she does not decide to do something about it *today*, you have lost a sale.

The prospect may imply, or you may infer, that he or she will buy "someday." But someday is rather like tomorrow: it never comes. And from the prospect's point of view, why should it? Put yourself in his or her shoes. Would you pay a year's utility bills in advance (assuming you received no discount for doing so)? Would you go out and buy a new window pane because your son has started playing baseball, or would you wait until the inevitable took place first? Would you lend your brother $1,000 because, even though things are going fine for him now, who knows, he might get laid off next month? Of course not.

People do not do today what they can put off to tomorrow. That is why the stores are crowded with last minute shoppers the day before Christmas.

That is why young newlyweds have a difficult time thinking about retirement planning. That is why most red-blooded Americans who owe additional taxes file as close to the April 15 deadline as possible. Everyone knows Christmas falls on December 25th. Everyone knows he or she will grow old and want to retire someday. And everyone knows that taxes are inevitable and must be paid by April 15th.

At the same time, if you have done an effective job of selling up to this point, your prospects know that they have a problem or a need. And they know what they should do about it ... someday. Your task is to turn that "someday" into "today." And you do that by consciously, actively, deliberately (and sometimes persistently) closing the sale, or selling the sale.

One word of explanation here. In a typical sales situation, closing will come at this stage of the interview, following the presentation of the solution. However, this is not to say that it will always take place just that way. That is because while all sales are similar, no two are exactly alike and rarely are they "typical." If the prospect shows signs of wanting to seal the deal earlier, do not look a gift horse in the mouth. It is not unheard of for inexperienced salespeople -- interrupted during their presentations because the prospect wants to conclude the sale -- to insist on finishing the presentation first. With that, they may very well talk the prospect out of a sale.

Once again, use common sense. Also, look for what are known as "buying signals." Examples of buying signals include the following types of questions from prospects:

- *"What kind of payment plans are available?"*

- *"Does that come with a guaranteed renewable option?"*

- *"Do I have to take a physical to qualify?"*

- *"You say I can get a discount if I pay the entire amount now. What kind of discount are we talking about?"*

And there are others. Most buying signals take the form of (1) detailed interest in some aspect of the product itself; (2) questions about methods of payment or financing arrangements; or (3) questions about types of service and terms of contract renewal. If the prospect begins sending out buying signals, move immediately to the close. Do not hesitate, dawdle, fool around, or insist on completing your absolutely wonderful sales presentation. For one reason or another, your prospect is already sold on what you are selling. Do not keep him or her waiting.

The simplest and most obvious way to close the sale is simply to *ask* for it. This may sound obvious to you, but you would be amazed how many salespeople do everything perfectly up to that point: introduce themselves and establish genuine rapport with the prospect; masterfully identify needs and make prospects so aware of them that they actually begin showing outward signs of stress; present their product as the one, the only, the best solution to meet that need. Then, for some reason, they stop cold, wrap up with some less-than-distinctive comment like, "Well, what d'ya think, huh?" and wait for something to happen.

What is the prospect supposed to do? Suddenly a bucket of cold water has been poured on the interview. Imagine a fellow spending an entire evening wining and dining the woman of his dreams, buying her flowers, taking her to the fanciest restaurant in town, telling her that he has never met another woman like her, and that he wants her to be with him always, that he wants to make their relationship permanent. But he neglects to come out and actually ask her to marry him. It may sound awfully close to a proposal. But she'll be darned if she is going to ask for confirmation. So ask! Do not make the prospective buyer have to query you: "Can I buy it now?" Send out clear signals that say, "You should buy this … and you should buy it now."

The most important point about closing is to ask for the sale. Second only to that is the *way* you ask the prospect to buy. Your tone, your manner, your attitude should all say that you expect the prospect to buy, that to buy is the assumed, logical thing to do.

I was once actively involved in youth soccer and was the director of referees in our local association. Like myself, most of the referees were parents who volunteer, but who nonetheless had to be trained, state certified and willing to devote a major chunk of their weekends in the fall and spring. Realizing that their time was as valuable as mine, I was at first rather hesitant about asking these people to give up an evening at home to attend a referee clinic or meeting. The phone conversation would go something like this: "Ed, sorry to bother you, but we're holding a referees' meeting next Monday evening at the school. I know you're busy. But if at all possible, I'd appreciate it if you could attend. Now, if you can't, no problem; just let me know. I'll have Pat call you and fill you in on what happened."

My meetings were famous for no-shows. Why? Because I was making it absolutely clear that the world was not going to end if my referees did not attend. In fact, I was telling them that not coming was okay, that someone else who was dumb enough to attend would be able to summarize it all in a phone call. I was giving the impression that the meeting was neither necessary nor important.

Finally becoming aware of what I had been doing, I began changing my approach to those meetings. My tone became positive and firm: "Ed, we are having a meeting of all the referees next Monday evening. We will be covering some important rule changes and new procedures affecting the under-12-year-old teams. Since you will be refereeing games in that age division next weekend, it is very important that you attend." Attendance? It was rarely lower than 95% after that, compared to a 50% to 75% rate under my previous "please-come-if-you-absolutely-can't-find-something-better-to-do" approach.

My point is that you should not end your presentation with something downbeat: "Well, there it is. Do you think you'd like to buy it? I mean, you can think it over if you like, you know." You would certainly not use those exact words. However, if you show indecisiveness, if you give the impression that the purchase of this product is strictly an *optional* decision, chances are you're throwing away the sale. Your whole presentation up to this stage has been to point out to the prospect just how much he or she needs this product. Do not turn around at the moment of truth, when the buying decision is about to be made, and inject doubt or suggest that all this has been fun but is not really all that important.

So, work to bring the sale to a close, a positive close. Or as some sales managers stress, "Close and close often." This means that you should not expect to get the sale the first time you ask for it. People will resist being sold, so you should anticipate objections and handle them as they arise. If there are problems, they should have come out by this time. And if further objections are voiced, they can be addressed. (We will delve into that subject in greater detail in Chapter Eight, "Dealing with Objections."

As a general rule of thumb, you should attempt to close no less than three times, more if it seems warranted. The worst the prospect can do is say no. Expect some resistance. At the same time, however, expect the prospect to buy. To some degree, you can even assume, since he or she has stayed with you this far, that an agreement to purchase may be *implied*. Assume that the prospect has, in fact, made the decision to buy.

Here are some closing techniques that utilize this concept of *implied consent:*

- *Begin filling out the application or order form,* starting with easy questions, such as: "What is your phone number?" "Is the full name of the company the same as I have down here?" "What are the ages of your children?" If there are any additional questions or concerns on the part of the prospect, they will come out at this point. Otherwise, keep moving. If questions do come up, simply take the time to answer them and then return to the application.

- *Ask secondary questions,* such as questions involving payment method or delivery address. You skip over "Will you buy?" and go right to "How much?" or simply "How?" Here is how it might come out in practice:

    "I feel this plan is perfect for you, don't you agree (continuing to obtain the prospect's agreement and helping him make "small" decisions throughout the interview and helping put him in a 'yes' mood)? The only question now is, how much coverage do you need. Ideally, $700,000 would cover your family, safely, protecting Rita and your children if anything should happen to you. Maybe they could get by with a lesser amount, but I can't recommend it. So, should we go for the $700,000?"

    or

    "Would you like the to pay by check or credit card?"

- *Point out possible results of delaying.* What might happen if your prospect does not act, does not make a decision to buy *now?*

    "Most of all, you are young enough virtually to guarantee that, given present interest assumptions, you will be affluent in your retirement. But every day you delay will make it that much more difficult to accomplish that."

    "Let's make a rather morbid assumption. Let's say you died tonight. With this plan I am recommending, your family's financial security will be guaranteed. Without it, they will have to rely on a lot of luck and possibly the generosity of friends. You don't want that to happen, do you?"

"Right now, today, you can sign up for this policy and be assured coverage at these rates. But you can't guarantee that a year from now or six months from now or even next week, you'll be in the same good physical condition."

Step Five: Obtaining Referrals

Once you have closed the sale, do not take the money and run. And even if the prospect declines to make a buying decision (translation: a flat out "no"), the interview should not end yet. If you have done your job right, even if you have not made the sale, the prospect should feel positively about you, your sales style and methods, and the way you conducted yourself. You will never find a better person from whom to obtain referrals than someone who has just purchased your product or your service. The second best referrer is a prospect who has *not* purchased your product or your service, but has, nonetheless, been introduced to you and your business. Nine times out of ten, unless you have somehow managed to antagonize the prospect who does not buy from you, he or she will experience a twinge of guilt at having wasted your time and is even inclined to feel somewhat obligated to you. Take ten minutes at the end of the interview to ask for referrals. Make this a part of your sales presentation. Treat this step with importance, not as an afterthought, but as an integral part of your sales presentation. For more details on obtaining referrals, review the material in Chapter Four, "Prospecting."

The Ideal Sales Presentation

In this chapter, we have covered the organized sales presentation:

1. The approach/introduction (Selling Yourself)

2. Identification of problems or needs (Selling the Need/Problem)

3. Presentation of the solution (Selling the Solution)

4. Closing (Selling the Sale)

5. Obtaining referrals

These five elements are at the heart of every sales presentation. This is what all the preparation and planning is about. In that respect, this chapter is the core or heart of this book. If you master the steps we have covered here and learn to apply them to your own sales interviews, you will become increasingly more proficient as a sales professional and increasingly successful in your career.

But your job as a sales professional is not done yet. What we have covered in this chapter is the "ideal" sales situation, the open-and-shut interview during which you obtain data and information from your prospect while he or she listens and agrees with everything you suggest.

Unfortunately, the ideal only takes place in fairy tales. No matter how well prepared you may be, there is always the possibility that your prospect is going to ignore common sense, miss the point, or just flat out say "NO!" What to do when a prospect objects to your proposal is the subject of the next chapter.

Chapter Eight

Dealing with Objections

When I first became a manager in the corporate world, like most new managers, I had a rather unclear vision of just what a manager did. While continuing to write and produce training programs and industrial videos, I also took up the task of "managing." I tracked production and manufacturing details of my products, planned new products, mapped out workable schedules for bringing them on line by deadline, and delegated projects to a small but highly competent staff of subordinates. And all along the way, I ran into a continuous, though not overwhelming, array of problems. I would go home some evenings and lament that "This job wouldn't be so bad if it weren't for all those annoying problems that keep coming up."

Then one day, I realized that the problems were not really interfering with my job. Dealing with problems *was* my job. I had failed to see the forest for the trees. That realization put things into perspective for me. I began to see those annoying, daily problems as challenges. I studied problem patterns and began anticipating many in advance and heading them off before they ever materialized. I began planning for the unexpected. I began planning for the problems.

What does the above little anecdote have to do with selling? Plenty. What we described in Chapter Seven was an ideal sales presentation in which prospect and sales professional both played their parts and cooperated fully. If I were making the ideal sales situation into a movie, the description in the treatment would look like this:

"Open with prospect skeptical, sales pro enthusiastic, positive. Through application of proper sales techniques, sales pro begins to win over skeptical prospect. By the end, prospect has bought everything and supplies sales pro with 3,000 qualified referred leads."

However, if you have been on this earth for more than a week or two, you already know that the ideal exists only in training films and one's own imagination. Problems are a reality, a reality you must be prepared to face. The biggest problem you can expect to encounter is that of a prospect saying "no." It may emerge disguised as "I'd really like to think it over first," or "I purchased something similar from a competitor of yours just last week" or "I don't think we can swing it right now" or "I usually go through my brother." But no matter what the words may be, they add up to one and only one thing -- the prospect is saying NO!

When that happens, you have two choices. One is to pack up your tent and move on. The second is to stick around a little while longer and find out what the prospect really means -- if in fact he or she means "no" or if he or she only needs more information or some other reason to say "yes." If you are going to be successful in sales, you had better select choice number two.

Putting Objections in Perspective

You have just made a great presentation, the best in your life. You were suave, silver-tongued, totally in control. Everything went perfectly. But when you attempted to close the sale, something went wrong. The prospect said, "It sure sounds great, BUT.... And with that, you have just crossed the line from the ideal into the real. You have just received what is known in the business of selling as an objection. Objections can be genuine concerns or questions, excuses or evasions, or just indifference.

Objections are typical. They are common. Everybody gets them. They are to be expected. Handling them is a major part of your role as a sales professional. But take heart. The fact is that objections are not really all that bad. That's right. *Objections are normal, necessary signs of interest, which, when handled correctly, can actually lead to sales.*

So, in this respect, objections really are not bad. In fact, they are good. They are signs that the prospect is paying attention. Think of objections as feedback, as questions. They also provide you with something to work with. Imagine a sales presentation during which your prospect simply sits quietly and does not say one word. You have no idea what she is thinking . . . whether she agrees, disagrees, understands what you are saying, or is even paying attention at all.

But when a prospect raises an objection, saying something like, "I'm sorry, but I can't afford it," you have something solid to sink your teeth into. Maybe the mode of payment is the problem. Perhaps the prospect simply just does not see the need, which means you now can go back and explain it again. Even if he says, "I'm just not interested," you now can inquire further. The questions, "Why do you say that?" or "May I ask why?" may be all it takes to reveal a concern that can be easily addressed and overcome.

The real problems are cold silence and vague, noncommittal agreement. I have friends who are hopelessly addicted to their techno-gizmos. They will rattle on about internet and computer subjects about which I have no knowledge and less interest. Nonetheless, I try to smile agreeably and say things like, "Oh, really? That's really something." They think we are communicating. They think I understand what they are talking about. Salespeople sometimes have the same problem with their prospects. Sometimes the prospects do not really understand what is being said. Sometimes, they do not agree with what is being said, but are too polite to say so.

To uncover the problem of mindless agreement or tacit disagreement, many sales professionals *refuse* to accept silence from their prospects. In a nonthreatening way, they probe and question prospects to bring possible problem areas out in the open. They seek objections. Rather than viewing them as obstacles to sales, they see them as stepping stones that -- when handled properly -- calm prospects' fears, answer their questions, and bring the sale that much closer.

The most important thing to remember when attempting to put objections into perspective is not to be afraid of them. Instead of looking at them as problems, view them as opportunities to clear up any confusion on the prospect's part.

Most of all, when you do get objections, do not always take them at face value. If a prospect says, "I'm not interested," he or she may or may not mean it. Your job is to find out which. Whatever you do, do not simply walk away, because you may be walking away from a prospect who really was quite interested, in spite of what may have been said.

Also, keep in mind that there are some valid objections. If a prospect really cannot afford your product or really does not need or want it, that is a valid objection. Nothing you can say or do -- outside of some questionable sales tactics, which will always catch up to you sooner or later --will change that. But you should find out for sure before letting the subject drop and letting the prospect go.

An objection may be the result of a communication problem, a misunderstanding between you and the prospect. At other times you will encounter prospects who do not like to be thought of as "easy sales." Regardless of how much they may like what you have to offer, they have to give you a run for your money. Sometimes they want to find out how much you know about your own product, putting you through a kind of test before they commit themselves to buy from you. At other times, they may want to be sure they are getting the best deal, that the price is not too high or that you have not been leading with your high-priced product when a less costly version will do just as well.

You have probably witnessed it a thousand times . . . or even indulged in it. Americans are proud of their ability to horse trade. When I am selling a car through the newspaper and a prospective buyer comes out to look it over, I make a brief presentation on the status of the car and its features. Then I stand back and shut up. Naturally, the more questions the prospective buyer asks, the more interested he is. But when a prospect asks a lot of questions at first and then begins finding a number of things wrong with the car, I know he is close to buying. The ones who look, nod and walk away without saying anything except, "What are you asking for it?" are the ones who surprise me if they buy. And when we finally get around to talking money, I have never yet met a buyer who offered me the full asking price. If one did, I would know I had under-priced the car.

This is all part of an elaborate American buying game. "If I pay cash, do I get 5% off?" "I don't want it without the full five-year warranty." Americans love to horse trade. And to some, the game is more important than the outcome. So, when you attempt to work with them, they want to play. They will raise objections, question the quality of your product or the value they are getting for the dollar. Accept it. Unless you are selling snake oil, responsible consumers are nothing to be afraid of. They help you keep on your toes and continue to sharpen your sales skills.

However, when a prospect raises an objection, you have no way of telling whether that person is horse-trading or deadly serious. And if he or she is serious, you have no way of telling whether that person is fully aware of the facts or perhaps has misunderstood something in your presentation. The trick is to find out. And the best way to do that is to use a little persistence. One good rule of thumb is *never to accept the first two objections without question*. That means only after the third objection -- at the very least -- should you consider walking away from the sale. In other words, make at least three attempts to close.

Salesperson: *"It's as simple as that. Now, I need your date of birth for the application."*

Prospect: *"I'm sorry. We just can't afford it."*

Salesperson: *"I understand. Perhaps we might want to look at reducing the amount slightly to bring it more in line with your budget, to, say, $400,000 instead of $500,000, even though you really do need the full half a million dollars of coverage. Even so, you will need a medical examination. Would you prefer that I set it up for Thursday or Friday?"*

Prospect: *"I don't know. Even that way, the premium is still pretty high."*

Salesperson: *"I can see where it may be a bit steep all in one chunk. Let's set it up on a quarterly premium basis."*

Prospect: *"Yes, that would be better."*

Later in this chapter we will provide you with some effective responses to objections. But now let's examine another point in terms of putting and keeping objections in perspective. And that is the all-important matter of attitude. In spite of what you now know about objections, you may still be tempted to take them personally. It never makes you feel good when a prospect says no. However, objections are not a reflection upon you as an individual. Nor do they reflect your prospect's opinion of you. Never let objections affect you personally.

Turning Objections into Sales

Now that we have objections in their proper perspective, let's see what we can do about overcoming them. There are four possible strategies:

1. *Anticipate.* Military tacticians believe "the best defense is a good

offense." It is the same way in sales. The best way to answer most objections is to anticipate and respond to them in advance. As many possible objections as you can put to rest during the course of your presentation, the better. In fact, a good organized sales presentation does just that. Try to anticipate the prospect's initial suspicions and gear your presentation accordingly. Based on experience with other prospects, you may know that one feature or aspect of your product or service sometimes raises questions; with a little planning, you can head them off at the pass and answer them before they arise.

Historically, the one objection that consistently knocks sales professionals out of the batter's box is the "I-can't-afford-it" objection. And that is a tough one to overcome, unless you anticipate it in advance and defuse it before it becomes an issue. This can be done during and as a part of the presentation, depending upon the nature of the product, by either (1) establishing an acceptable or affordable dollar figure going in, or (2) selling dollar savings ("This will save you enough money to actually pay for itself in one year").

In consumer and financial services areas, establishing an acceptable or affordable dollar figure is the choice of most sales professionals. Note that when you go into most retail stores, the salesperson will ask what price range you have in mind. In financial services sales, this approach may be a bit different. But early in the interview, the conversation may go something like this:

> Salesperson: *"Before we begin, let me ask you a question. If you decide that a plan I may propose is right for you, could you afford to set aside, say, $200 a month to make it work for you?"*

> Prospect: *"No, I'm afraid that would be out of the question."*

> Salesperson: *"I understand. Of course, this helps me design a plan to*

meet your needs. Is $150 a feasible figure?"

Prospect: *"Not really. $100 is more like it."*

In many business situations, the "I-can't-afford-it" objection may often be overcome by selling the dollar savings on your program. This then becomes a part of your presentation, emphasizing that the prospect may very well not be able to afford *not* to act on your recommendation.

More specifically, you can often anticipate objections based on actual information you possess about certain prospects. For instance, they may be previous buyers or referrals. However, even if you are dealing with total strangers, you can anticipate a number of typical objections in advance. That is because, on the whole, there are only a handful of different types of objections you will ever hear. And if you know that a certain objection is likely to surface, heading it off in advance and answering it in your own words, not only defuses the objection, but at the same time demonstrates to your prospects that you understand their problems and concerns.

So, when at all possible, try to anticipate objections before they arise. Do this by preparing your presentation to answer as many potential objections before they come up, and also by having on hand an assortment of prepared responses. In the last section of this chapter are listed some common objections, along with suggested responses and guidelines for developing responses.

2. *Respond Indirectly.* A second method of dealing with objections is to respond indirectly. This is not the same as responding evasively. But it harkens back to our earlier discussion about not taking every objection at face value. For instance, suppose a prospect raises a series of objections designed to pull you hopelessly off course if you tried to

answer each one as they came up. Instead, you might suggest that he or she hold all questions for the moment, with the promise that you will return to them later in the interview. Often the question is covered during the normal course of your presentation. Or if the prospect was just horse-trading and the objection was not serious to begin with, chances are that it will not surface again.

What if a sales professional receives an objection before he had even begun his presentation? Consider the following:

Prospect: *"I want you to know right up front that I think cash value life insurance is a big rip-off."*

Salesperson: *"There are some people who prefer term insurance. If we conclude that you do need additional coverage, I'll be glad to discuss the different types of policies and we can see which one is right for you. But let's first see if you even have a need, okay?"*

If the agent in the above example had let himself be pulled into a debate of permanent versus term coverage (which is pretty much what the prospect was hoping would happen), the presentation might never have gotten back on track. But the agent managed to keep the subject on target and at the same time remind the prospect that he may have been a bit hasty in assuming his own need, thereby demonstrating to the prospect his integrity and interest in meeting serving the prospect's best interest, not simply selling products.

A second indirect response to objections, most effective with those you are certain are just at all real, is to ignore the objection altogether. In response to deliberately dumb or silly objections, try the silent treatment. The prospect has tried to put the ball in your court by making some inane remark to see how you will react. But you do not have to return the serve; you do not have to play along with the prospect's game. By being patient and waiting out the prospect, sometimes you get to what is really troubling him:

> Prospect: *"I think life insurance is stupid. (silence) You get a fat commission check. The companies get rich. But we just pay and pay. You have to die to win. (silence) It's just that it's a gamble, right? (silence) Well, what do you think?"*

> Salesperson: *"The purpose of insurance is protection. I think you need the coverage, and I believe this plan is right for you."*

> Prospect: *"Yeah, but the premium's a bit stiff."*

> Salesperson: *"Well, let's look at some of the options open to us.*

3. *Respond Directly.* Some objections require a direct response at the time they are raised. They represent serious, well-thought-out questions or concerns and they should not be ignored, put off or treated lightly. Take them seriously. Perhaps they are the result of a misunderstanding over some point in your presentation. Perhaps they are simply requests for additional information. When such serious objections surface, they deserve straightforward, direct responses.

Assuming the product you are recommending is right for that person's needs, there are essentially three types of direct responses you can offer:

First, restate the objection: By restating the objection in your own words, you are not only responding directly to your prospect's question, but you are also able to phrase your response in such a way that it helps the prospect see the question or objection from a different, possibly clearer, perspective. For instance:

Prospect: *"The problem is that the cost is simply too high."*

Salesperson: *"If I understand you correctly, you're saying the total, single lump-sum price is beyond your reach. I agree. But let's look at it the way we'd look at a house purchase, in terms of monthly installments. Now, if we spread the cost several years...."*

Second, take the "yes-but" approach. The "yes-but" (or "diplomatic but firm") direct response is ideal for correcting strongly held misconceptions without offending your prospect. You agree with what the prospect says, and then go on to point out the error. For instance:

Prospect: *"I feel that what I presently have is just fine already."*

Salesperson: *"Oh, I agree that you can get by with what you have ... for today. But every day that passes puts your present situation and your changing needs further and further apart. There will never be a better time to change that than right now."*

Third, take the "Hit 'em between the eyes" approach. If you are talking to a friend, someone you have known a long time, or a prospect who you have sized up as being a no-nonsense straight shooter who appreciates candor, this may be the best way to deal with objections. While you should never ridicule a person's question or objection, do not be afraid to say, "I'm sorry to have to tell you this, but you're flat out wrong," or "No, *you* may not need this, but we're not talking about you; we're talking about your family."

This approach also is quite effective as a kind of shock treatment when all other methods of dealing with objections have failed and you get the impression the prospect is more or less playing a devil's advocate role with you, raising objections for their own sake:

Salesperson: *"Look, here it is. We both know you need it. There is nothing more I can say. The decision is now yours"* (laying the application in front of the prospect and waiting, pen in hand).

Determining Which Approach to Use

The techniques we have just discussed for dealing with objections have all proven their effectiveness over the years. However, one may be better than another for any given prospect or situation. Which one is right brings us back once again to common sense.

Naturally, you will want to anticipate as many objections as possible in advance. But when an objection does come up, you must decide whether to take a direct or an indirect response. There are no patent answers. However, following are some factors you may wish to consider:

- *The mood of the interview.* If everyone is relaxed and feeling comfortable with one another, a more direct response may be in order. However, if you are having a difficult time establishing a relationship with your prospect, if there is a formal stiffness in the air, be more discreet, more sensitive to the possibility of alienating the prospect.

- *Your relationship with the prospect.* Naturally, you will tend to be more direct and informal with a close friend or relative. And a referred lead will be easier to deal with more directly than will a cold call you have never met before.

- *The attitude of the prospect.* If a prospect casually throws out an objection with a shrug, you might respond differently than if he or she sits back for a moment and, looking you straight in the eye, asks a carefully worded, well-thought-out question. A serious response to the first may be as deadly as a whimsical answer to the second.

- *The nature of the objection.* An objection about the soundness of an entire financial program is different than an objection about the mode of payment or a question about future service. An objection on a major point may require a careful, detailed explanation. On the other hand, an objection over a detail may often be dispatched rather quickly.

Most of all, treat every objection seriously in your own mind. Yes, you may choose to ignore it with the prospect. That is because, if you miss an objection or do not think it is worth taking seriously, it could cost you the sale.

A Sampling of Commonly Raised Objections

With objections in proper perspective and a mastery of the techniques used to handle them, you are now ready to familiarize yourself with an inventory of some of the most common objections you can expect to encounter in a sales situation. Following are three of the most likely objections, along with one or more possible responses.

1. *"Sorry, but I'm just not interested."* "All right. But could you be a bit more specific? Could you tell me exactly what it is about this product which leaves you feeling that way?" (If you get no specific response, continue to probe, reviewing specific aspects of your presentation. If you are then able to obtain a specific response, review that section of your presentation again, followed by another closing attempt.)

2. *"I can't afford it."* "I can understand your saying that. But let's look at it another way. Your industry is getting increasingly competitive. Can your business really afford *not* to have this?" (Close with details of alternative to not buying.)

   or

   "If this is really right for you — and I believe it is — we do have several options." (Present different payment alternatives or suggest reducing amount.)

3. *"Not right now. See me later."* "If you want to wait, that's up to you. I might add, however, that delaying the purchase may end up costing you more at a later time."

or

"I'm afraid I'm a bit confused. We agree that what I'm recommending is what you need, right?" (If the answer is yes, then proceed as follows.) "Then my coming back in a few days or weeks should have nothing to do with your decision. So, why don't we take care of it now? It not only saves me another trip back, but we can get your program in the works now, giving you the benefit immediately." (If the response is no, ask for specifics and deal with those objections accordingly.)

These are just three objections and possible responses. They are included to demonstrate that there is no reason for you to stand with your mouth open when a prospect raises an objection. You should prepare responses to specific objections. In fact, you should keep an "Objection File." Whenever you encounter a new objection, or at least one that is new to you, write it down and file it.

Objection:

Response:

Effectiveness:

Alternate Response:

If you keep an Objection File containing objections and responses, and if you continue to refine that file and make sure you know your responses, you will soon have little trouble with objections, and accordingly, close more and more sales as a result.

But being able to close a sale and pocket a list of referrals does not end the sales process. Considering your task completed at that point would be a costly and unnecessary mistake. In the next chapter, we will look at another important aspect of the sales cycle: how to turn customers into clients and thereby build a business that continues to pay off year after year.

Chapter Nine

After the Sale –
Building Long-Term Business

As a sales professional, you must work hard to make sales. Nobody hands them to you. But every sale need not be a challenge. Once you have turned a prospect into a new buyer, you have already laid the groundwork for the next -- and much easier -- sale.

Perhaps you are familiar with the situation where a veteran sales professional sits back in his office and conducts business over the phone. Going through his files, he dials a number and spends a few minutes chatting with a client who is more like an old friend than a customer. During the course of the conversation, he talks about a new product or suggests that it is time for another annual review. He may even make the sale over the phone. If he does go out on a call, he is welcomed like an old friend of the family or a cherished business adviser. The sales interview itself is more like an after-dinner chat, during which the guest offers advice and suggestions to a very trusting client.

It is a beautiful picture. It is also a very real one for virtually all successful sales professionals. It can be the same for you as well, as long as you remember that the sales process does not end with a sale. In fact, it should never end. One of your objectives should be to turn every one-time buyer into a long-term client. The saying, "A bird in the hand is worth two in the bush," illustrates perfectly the value of establishing long-term relationships and distinguishes the term "client" from "buyer."

It is through this type of repeat, long-term business that true success comes in the sales world. Establishing yourself with clients who you go back to year after year is how you build your business in the truest sense. The sales professional who cultivates buyers, who converts this year's buyers into next year's clients, is like the apple farmer who invests as much as a decade planting, cultivating and developing an orchard of healthy trees, receiving very little return for his effort during those early years. Once the trees are finally of a fruit-bearing age, he continues to tend them, each year harvesting a new crop of apples. Getting in that first year's crop is the most difficult. But after that, once the trees are established and in full production, the work is primarily in the nature of maintenance. And that orchard will continue to bear fruit for years to come.

Just as the apple farmer would not harvest his first year's crop and then move on to plant another brand-new orchard and leaving the old one behind, the successful sales professional would not think of making a sale to a buyer this year, never to return again. Not only would it be a disservice to the buyer (for if the salesperson did a good job, the buyer will look forward to continuing service, to doing business with that person again in the future), but it would be like going hungry while the fruit grows ripe on the tree. It is for this very reason that you must learn to view a sale to a new prospect not as *the* sale, but as the *first* sale. Following that first sale and by providing ongoing service to your new client will help bring in sale after sale after sale year after year after year.

Ongoing service is the key to long-term success. Ongoing service is what makes your job profitable. The value of working with existing clients is that, each year, the selling becomes easier. It is not long before you are able to sell more in less time than you had thought possible.

Let's use our sample goal of 300 sales in one year as an example. Assume that every one of those sales in the first year was to a stranger. Your sales ratio was 10-3-1 (ten prospects to three appointments to one sale). The next year, you make 300 sales again. However, only 250 of them are new prospects. The other 50 are buyers from last year. You may notice that while your 10-3-1 ratio still holds for new buyers, that ratio should be much better when dealing with people who bought from you the year before. For purposes of illustration, let's say that half the previous buyers you called granted you appointments and half of those bought from you again. That puts your ratio for these people at *10-5-2.5,* which is a 250% *increase* over your productivity with new prospects. So, right away, your second year was a bit easier than your first.

But let's keep going. At the end of two years, you should have *550* buyers' names in your files (the first year's buyers and the 250 new buyers from the second year). Of course, realistically, due to attrition, you will have lost some existing buyers a year for one reason or another. Let's put that figure at 50 a year. So at the end of two years, you have a file of 450 active buyers. Each year, you add 250 new names, sell 50 existing buyers, and lose *50.* Let's make one more assumption and say that your objective is to have an active file of 1,000 names. Well, at the end of five years, you have 1,050 names. In theory, after that, you only need 50 new buyers each year to replace the 50 you lost through attrition. Of course, you may actually lose more than that. Nonetheless, before you know it, you are working like that veteran we described a few paragraphs ago.

Post-Sale Activity

How do you turn this year's buyers into next year's clients? There are a number of things you can do, and they all fall under the heading of "post-sale activity." As the name implies, post-sale activity means that you do not simply take the money after the sale is made and run for the hills. You tend to the needs of your new buyer, making sure that everything is as it should be, standing behind your product and beside your new client long after that first commission check has been spent. Post-sale activity means serving as your own customer service department, taking personal responsibility for your client's satisfaction.

This is as it should be if you are serious about turning buyers into long-term clients. Do not develop the attitude that you are selling a product and nothing more. There are plenty of competitive products around. And remember, if products sold themselves, there would be no need for you. Fundamentally, there is really not much difference between a Ford and a Chevrolet, or a Honda and a Toyota. And people base their loyalties to one or the other of these fine automobiles on two things: the overall trouble-free miles they had with the last one they bought and the friendliness and quality of service they received from the dealer. Do not simply sell a product. Sell your services and be the person who provides products and makes sure that all goes well.

Note the difference in personal quality service between a fine restaurant and a fast food chain. Both provide food. But that is where the similarities stop. The fast food chain offers an acceptable basic standard of quality and operates on volume. Contrary to what the teenager behind the counter might say, nobody really cares whether or not you have a nice day. And even if you patronized that same restaurant every day for a year, chances are good that nobody would greet you by name. You are and will remain just an order pick-up number.

The fine restaurant, on the other hand, specializes in nothing but personalized service. The waiter and maitre de pride themselves on remembering your name, that you prefer your coffee with your meal, that you like the table by the window, and so on. They treat you better than your own mother ever did, making you feel that you are their only customer. And that is why you go back. Sure, the food may be good. But most of all, you're greeted personally and made to feel like a million bucks. The secret is that the people make you feel special. They make you feel important and cared about. The prices may be higher than at the fast food outlet, but the service is what is memorable.

Essentially, that is what *you* must do: make your service memorable. The results will be well worth the effort. Not only will it help guarantee that today's sale stays sold, but it will lead to strong referrals and more future business than you can shake a stick at. And it really is not all that difficult.

Once the sale is made, there are three phases of your post-sale activities, which will turn those buyers into clients: product delivery, critical point contact and periodic follow-up. Let's take a look at each.

Product Delivery

Product delivery is a crucial point in the sale. Between the time of the sale and the time the goods are placed in the buyer's hands, the buyer has had a chance to entertain serious second thoughts. Psychologists refer to this as "buyer remorse," and it is a fairly common occurrence. "Should I have spent the money?" "Have I shopped around enough?" "Should I have thought about it longer?" "Is this really what I need?" These are the types of questions that go through the buyer's mind after the deal is closed. By the time everything is ready for delivery, the buyer may have convinced him or herself that a terrible mistake was made and decide to call every-thing off.

That is why it is so important to be there at delivery. In spite of a desire to avoid the delivery process altogether — mail the insurance policy, let customer service install the new equipment, hide in the back room, etc. — it is crucial that you do everything possible to insure delivery in person.

Think of the delivery as a second selling interview. The buyer may have forgotten why this purchase was such a good idea. If the buyer appears to have undergone a change of heart, you may wish to review the key features and benefits once again. Not only does this solidify the initial sale, but it also helps sell you to the buyer. It's a sad commentary on the image held by many about salespeople, but consumers in America almost expect hit-and-run tactics. The salesman loves you, is your best friend ... until he has your money. Then he is too busy even to look at you. By making delivery in person you have already gone a lot further than most salespeople. You are following up, making sure everything is as was agreed, taking care of your new client.

Product delivery is also the ideal time to prospect. You have delivered the product. The buyer has had all questions and concerns taken care of. There's no better time to ask for the names of others who might benefit from what you have to offer.

What if you cannot be there in person? First of all, there are very few reasons why you cannot. If you are selling insurance products, you should schedule delivery at a time when you are available to do it in person. If equipment or a new service is being installed from your home office, find out when delivery is scheduled and make every effort to be there when it arrives, or no less than a day after. However, if you absolutely cannot be there in person, be there in spirit. Call shortly before scheduled delivery and then again after delivery is expected, letting the customer know that you are there to help if there is a problem of any kind and that you are only a phone call or email away.

By being conscientious and making yourself available once the sale is made, you will position yourself within the buyer's mind as a caring, conscientious professional and you will be remembered with gratitude. And after all that, where is that buyer going to turn the next time he or she needs a product or service that you can provide? And who will he or she tell friends or business associates about when they mention such a need? You bet: YOU!

Critical Point Contact

Delivery lays the groundwork for future sales. But even with your personalized attention at this point, the buyer does not necessarily regard him or herself as your client. To begin changing that, you will want to make contact again within a few months of the initial sale. In insurance sales, this critical point contact is known as the *critical premium contact* and should take place when the next premium comes due on the policy. This not only builds the relationship, but it also helps insure that the policy stays in force.

This critical point contact helps the buyer-client realize that you have every intention of being around for a long time to come, that you are reliable, that you are conscientious, that you stand behind what you sell and are always available when needed.

If you are in auto or equipment sales, the critical point contact may be at the time of the first scheduled service appointment or when it is estimated that the car has traveled 10 miles or the equipment has passed the 100 hour mark. Even if you are selling pencils or cookware, be in touch to make sure the customer is satisfied with your product and your service.

Periodic Follow-Up and Review

One of the primary objectives of post-sale activity is to make sure that your name stays in front of your clients. That is why it is so important to stay in touch. Here are some ways to maintain contact:

- *Establish a mailing list … and use it.* These days, you can send out an e-letter at the click of a button. The cost is almost nothing. Send it out periodically, such as monthly, and make sure it contains information of interest to your clients, not just sales info you want to promote.

- *Remember birthdays, anniversaries, and special occasions.* Send a birthday card to each client, as well as a Christmas or Seasons Greetings card. Also, point out special news items of personal importance to clients. For instance, if you have just read an article about a new breed of goldfish and know that one of your clients is a tropical fish enthusiast, take 60 seconds out of your life to clip the article, attach a short, handwritten note and send it. Do the same if you see a news item about your client, his or her company or a member of his or her family.

- *Serve as a clearinghouse for clients.* If one of your clients wholesales photocopy equipment and another is a retailer of office equipment and supplies, they may very well appreciate hearing from each other. Or perhaps two clients have similar hobbies or interests. You may not wish to do this uninvited, of course. However, if one client laments that she does not know where to go to get quality service on her car, you may tell her about another client who runs an auto repair shop. Be aware of such opportunities. They present themselves more often than you may realize. This is also known as networking, and it can boost your professional image among your client base.

- *Mix business and pleasure.* Socialize with your clients. If there is a natural affinity, have them over to dinner or share sports tickets with them. The only rule here is to stay away from subjects about business during social events. If it is necessary to discuss business, set aside several minutes beforehand, after which things should be kept strictly on a social level.

- *Get together in person at least once a year.* Over the course of a year you may phone or write a prospect three or four times. But it is important to call in person at least once a year. This is a formal, business call. During this interview, you will review the client's satisfaction with the previous purchase. But more than that, there are two very specific objectives of the meeting.

The first is to look for new sales opportunities. Perhaps needs have changed, situations have altered. You must be ready to meet those new needs and conduct a full presentation, leading up to a sale. This is the most enjoyable selling of all. A trusting relationship has already been established. All you need do is identify the need and provide your solution.

The second purpose is to obtain referrals. More than likely, the client is looking at you more and more as a friend. While he or she may have been reluctant to provide names for you at your first encounter, that person is now more than likely quite willing — perhaps eager — to provide a long list. Some sales professionals have reported that clients have on occasion actually given them their personal telephone books to take back to the office and copy at their leisure.

The Problem of Sales vs. Service

None of what we have been discussing in this chapter is really all that difficult. Yes, post-sale activity does take a little bit of effort, but it is effort that will pay off mightily in the long run. However, this is one of the most difficult things for a new salesperson to understand and carry out. Understandably so.

If you are a new salesperson, you are under a great deal of pressure to succeed. That success — both from your own and your company's point of view — is measured by the size of today's sales and today's commission checks. However, you cannot just think about today. If you are to be successful in your career, you must plan for the long haul. If you plan for tomorrow today, tomorrow will take care of itself.

The Whole Process

We have now completed the entire sales process. You will note that while there are a number of techniques and very specific activities you should do, there were no magic ingredients, secret formulas or special incantations. The entire sales process involves a great deal of hard work, common sense and practice.

However, there are a couple of additional ingredients, which will quite literally guarantee your success as a sales professional. They come as close to being magic ingredients as anything you will encounter in this life. We will discuss this in the final chapter.

Chapter Ten

The Magic Ingredients

Remember that overworked story about the tortoise and the hare? It may have been entertaining when you were a kid. It should have even more meaning now that you are an adult and embarking on a career in sales. Let's say both of these characters are sales creatures (as opposed to being sales *people)*. Both have mastered the fundamentals of selling and have exactly the same sales ability. In short, they are alike in their product knowledge and sales skills.

However, they are different in two ways. The tortoise possesses two magic ingredients, missing in the hare. It is because of these two ingredients that the hare was left sleeping by the tree while the tortoise won the race. Neither of these ingredients is luck. It has nothing to do with luck that the hare just happened to fall asleep. Just as that tortoise had to keep going against what appeared to be the most overwhelmingly hopeless odds, that wisecracking, know-it-all hare could not have finished that race if his life had depended upon it. He just did not have what it took to win the race. He lacked those two ingredients.

What did the tortoise have that the hare did not? What are those two magic ingredients? The first one is *an indomitable capacity for hard work.* The second is *a winning attitude.* Again, they are:

- *An indomitable capacity for hard work*

- *A winning attitude*

Regardless of any other factors, of any other conditions or circumstances, the man or woman who possesses these two ingredients will be successful in this career as a sales professional. These two ingredients are the beginning and the end of all accomplishment. Hard work and a winning attitude are what get you going, what bring you to the top . . . and what keep you there. These two ingredients far outstrip natural intelligence, education or social position when it comes to becoming successful.

We will discuss these two magic ingredients on the next several pages of this book. But before beginning, we would like to remind you that this chapter is not meant to be a complete work on the subject. That would require volumes of books. In fact, at the end of this chapter is a list of recommended reading so that you can pursue the subject further. This chapter is merely to serve as an introduction to you, since no book on selling would be complete without an emphasis on the importance of these two ingredients.

There Is No Substitute for Hard Work

Earlier we talked about time management and how to make the best use of your time. Now let's go one step further and see if you are willing to put in extra time — in the form of hard work — to become successful in your sales career. This means the first thing you should do is forget about everybody else's definition of "a full week's work." Each week consists of a total of 168 hours. On the average, people in this country count 35 hours as a normal workweek. They work five days a week, seven hours a day, and then "reward" themselves very often by doing as little as possible for the remaining 133 hours. They view work as the enemy, to be dispatched and gotten away from as quickly as possible. Their extra time is spent sleeping, watching television or socializing.

This approach to work may do just fine in a salaried job where you work for someone else and see no hope for improvement, or if you are receiving pay increases based on union negotiations rather than merit, or if you simply do not care about being successful. But as a sales professional, you must think differently about work. Admittedly, you do not want to devote all your waking time to your career. Your family, your hobbies, your leisure-time pursuits are important too. But at the same time you must evaluate your own definition of "a full week's work." Do you mean 35 hours a week? Forty hours? Or do you mean something else?

This is especially important in the crucial early years of a sales career. Putting in a 35-hour week will just not cut it. At the same time, be reasonable with yourself. Take one week and plan 60 hours worth of work. This may require getting up at 5 a.m. and putting in two early-bird hours on administrative work before the rest of the world stirs, followed by ten more hours during the day (including a working lunch with a prospect), which, let's say, puts you home by 7 p.m. Keep up this pace for one five-day week, and you have not only put in 60 hours (a better than 50% increase in activity which, we hope, will lead to at least a 50% or more increase in sales), but you have also earned a well-deserved weekend with the family. Then the next week you may drop down to 50 hours; then back up to 60 again the next.

Maintaining this pace requires discipline and devotion to your work. Remember, your career is not just a job. It is not just another activity, on the same level as cutting the grass or playing poker with friends. Your career is your primary activity, and you must treat it as such. You must be willing to do whatever it takes (within legal and moral limits, of course) to make your sales career as successful as you want it to be.

What this means is that there is no substitute for good old fashion hard work. Forget the flashy dancers and slick hotshots. Most of the supposed naturals in this business take off like a rocket and fizzle out fast. Be like the tortoise, not the hare. Dig in and just work hard. There are no substitutes for long, quality hours.

A Winning Attitude Makes You a Winner

It should be obvious by now that luck plays little, if any, part in an individual's ultimate success. Hard work is what keeps you going, keeps you learning, keeps you moving always toward your goals. But even more important than hard work as a success factor is your attitude. If you forgot everything you read in this book and even if you failed to learn anything at all about your product, you could still sell successfully if you had the right attitude, a winning attitude. In the words of Paul J. Meyer, super salesman and motivator of thousands, "You aren't enthusiastic because you make the sale. You make the sale because you're enthusiastic."

This is not to say that you can or should go charging out into the field armed only with hope in your soul. You should realize, however, that, if you are well-trained and well-prepared, and you add to that a positive, winning attitude, you will be downright unbeatable.

What do we mean by a winning attitude? It is more than just a hopeful smile plastered on your face or the emotional rush you get when your alma mater wins the big game of the season. It is also more than shallow hype. Some people mistakenly think they can motivate their salespeople, inject them with a dose of enthusiasm, with that winning attitude, by having them run around the room chanting, "I feel great."

Sorry. A winning attitude is the outward reflection of inner conviction and confidence. For that very reason, it is power itself. It is what pushes through against the odds, what keeps you going when the immediate facts indicate that you do not stand a chance. It is, once again, thinking like that tortoise who no one thought stood a chance but who never had the slightest doubt that he could win and that he *would* win.

Perhaps you doubt that attitude is the single most important ingredient in your road to success. That's understandable. The connection is not readily apparent to many people. So, let's see if we can put the subject into perspective.

Attitude is a function of the mind. It is to a great degree nothing more than how we perceive things. For instance, take a one-quart bottle of milk that has one pint of milk in it. To a person with a winning attitude, that bottle is half *full*. To a person without a winning attitude, it is half *empty*. With some things, it may not make a difference what you think. It will not change the facts. It will, however, change how you react to the facts. When it gets right down to it, attitude is just about everything.

For instance, take your own health. Worry, misery, and frustration can lead to nervous indigestion, tension, ulcers, even heart disease. These are mentally induced ailments. On the other hand, the person with a winning attitude does not worry needlessly, does not fret and become frustrated over setbacks, does not regret missed opportunities or passed glories. As a result, he or she is healthier, probably sleeps a lot better, and in the long run is a great deal happier.

Remember our early space program? When the USSR launched Sputnik in 1957, the U.S. program was going anywhere but up. In fact, there were standing jokes that our rockets always blew up. Sputnik sobered everyone up fast, and within a year the United States space program was on the right track. Its members developed what has come to be known as a "Can Do" mentality. And with that new attitude, the U.S. space program met or beat every goal it set. President John Kennedy promised in the early '60s that we would have men on the moon by the end of that decade. At the time, it seemed like a reckless claim. However, in July 1969, we launched Apollo XI and Neil Armstrong took that first historic step.

We did it with the right attitude. A winning attitude does not say it cannot be done. It says it *can* be done, and then figures out exactly how to do it.

As I mentioned, attitude is a product of the mind. And the mind is a very powerful tool. It is always working, carrying out what we program it to do. That is why, ultimately, we just about always get what we *really* want in this world. That's right. Because when you set your mind on something, it automatically begins working to obtain it for you; it automatically begins seeking out ways to accomplish your goals, whether they are conscious or subconscious.

The problem is that too many people have *negative* subconscious goals of which they are not even aware, fed by fear or guilt or lack of faith in themselves. For whatever reason, these people have locked onto failure and, as a result, have developed psychological and behavioral patterns that are directed by and aimed at failing. The truly unfortunate fact is that few of them understand this; few of them realize that they have the power to change the failure patterns, simply by planning for success. It's a matter of retuning one's thinking, recharting objectives and goals and programming the mind with a winning attitude.

A winning attitude will enable you to accomplish anything you set out to do. A winning attitude will open doors that you could not open otherwise. How? Mostly by contagion. Attitude is contagious. How we behave, how we appear, has a decided impact upon those around us.

Picture the following. You are attending the wedding of a distant relative. You really do not know anybody and are looking for the opportunity to ease your way into the social mainstream. What do you look for? A friendly, open face. One fellow walks into the hall. He looks sallow; his hands are stuffed into his pockets, his eyes somber and nervously casting about the room. He avoids eye contact and shuffles past you, his shoulders stooped. Behind him enters another fellow. But his head is erect, his eyes are alert. He has an agreeable smile on his face, and he walks with an air of a man who has purpose, who has confidence. The second his eyes meet yours, he smiles, shakes hands and introduces himself.

You have probably seen both kinds of people every day. Now think through the effect their actions and their attitudes have on you. The first fellow (the bride's father, perhaps?) presents a negative image. He certainly does not make you feel good. You will probably not seek him out for conversation later because he really does not seem like much fun to be with. In fact, he is probably quite depressing and will begin telling you about his latest operation two minutes into any conversation.

The second fellow, on the other hand, creates an instantly likable impression. He seems open, friendly. He appears to be genuinely interested in you. Based upon first impressions, you would prefer this fellow's company to the first man's.

It is as simple as that. People like being around positive people. They like doing business with them for the same reason. Attitude shows through in a person's tone of voice, posture, stride, facial expression and actions. And that attitude is contagious. In a selling situation, that translates quite easily into increased sales. If you are enthusiastic about what you are doing and what you are selling, the prospective buyer is going to pick up on that, and at the same time pick up some of that enthusiasm as well.

Developing a Winning Attitude

Some people seem to have been born with an inherently positive outlook on life, with an attitude that exudes confidence, enthusiasm and success. However, for the vast majority of us, our attitudes are as inconsistent as the winds of fortune in our lives. When something goes well, we feel good. When things go against us, we lose heart. Our attitude is buffeted by circumstance. And for some reason, left to its own devices, our attitude tends to the negative. While we are quick to see the bad, the negative, the unhappy, we often become blind to the good, the positive, the joyful.

The trick is to develop that positive side, to develop a winning attitude.

Anybody can do it. It is simply a matter of wanting to do so, along with
a willingness to devote yourself to a lot of hard work. Here are some
suggestions to get you on track.

- *Read* motivational and inspirational books. The titles of some of the
  finest, most inspired and inspiring books ever written by the world's
  greatest minds are provided for you at the end of this chapter. These
  books will not only teach you how to develop that winning attitude, but
  they will also help you restore an overall positive outlook on life. They
  can be powerful forces. Pick out any one of the books in the list that
  follows and set aside at *least* half an hour each day to work your way
  through it.

- *Set your goals.* Consciously chart your own career course and your own
  life course. Then keep your mind on exactly the things you do want and
  off the things you do not.

- *Develop "inspirational dissatisfaction."* Do not accept the non-attainment of
  your goals. Be dissatisfied with the way things are. Remember, people do
  get exactly what they *really* want. Do not aim too low. Do you want to
  double your sales? Do you want to double your income? You will if you
  really and genuinely want to.

- *Believe in what you are doing.* If you believe that what you are doing is
  illegal, immoral, or just not of any value, then you should immediately
  seek another direction, something you can believe in. Belief in what you
  are doing and what you are selling is a major factor in developing a
  winning attitude.

- *Grab yourself by the lapels.* In other words, make yourself totally
  responsible for the outcome of your life. Never play the victim. No
  exceptions. What you do with your life is not your parents' fault, the
  weather's fault, your manager's fault or just a matter of good or bad luck.

It is up to you. Accept no excuse from yourself. What you make of yourself is between you and yourself.

The Last Word

As you reach the end of this book, you should be aware that you have read (and hopefully learned) some of the most valuable information you will ever acquire. That is not an egotistical statement because few of the ideas in this book are mine. I wish I could claim them as original. They have been gathered over the years as a result of trial and error by sales professionals.

This book should be seen as a beginning, a starting point, which shoulders you in the direction of where you should go and what, you should do. This book alone will do nothing for you. Just reading it will make you a little more knowledgeable. But that is not enough.

Fishes swim. Singers sing. Writers write. And sales professionals sell. It is now up to you to take the ideas you have learned and turn them into action, turn them into sales.

Study your profession. Practice it. Make a point of improving yourself a little bit every day, of sharpening your skills, of honing your sales abilities a little more finely with every sales call. You'll soon reap the benefits that only the profession of selling can offer.

So work hard. Make money. Have fun. – John R. Ingrisano

RECOMMENDED READING

Alger, Horatio
> *Robert Coverdale's Struggle*

Autry, James
> *Love and Profit*
> *The Servant Leader*

Bennett, Arnold
> *How to Live on 24 Hours a Day*

Bettger, Frank
> *How I Raised Myself from Failure to Success in Selling*

Bienstock, Louis
> *The Power of Faith*

Brande, Dorthea
> *Wake Up and Live*

Canfield, Jack and Hansen, Mark Victor
> *Chicken Soup for the Soul*

Carnegie, Andrew
> *Autobiography of Andrew Carnegie*

Carnegie, Dale
> *How to Win Friends and Influence People,*
> *How to Stop Worrying and Start Living*

Clarke, Edwin L.
> *The Art of Straight Thinking*

Clason, George S.
> *The Richest Man in Babylon.*

Covey, Stephen R.
> *The 7 Habits of Highly Effective People,*
> *The 8th Habit: From Effectiveness to Greatness*

Douglas, Lloyd
> *Magnificent Obsession*

Franklin, Benjamin
> *The Autobiography of Benjamin Franklin*

Hansen, Mark Victor and Allen, Robert G
　　　　The One-Minute Millionaire
Hensley, Dennis E.
　　　　*The Power of Positive Productivity: Accelerate Your Success and
　　　　Create the Life You Want*
Hill, Napoleon
　　　　The Law of Success
　　　　Think and Grow Rich
　　　　Science of Success Course
Hill, Napoleon & Stone, W. Clement
　　　　Success Through a Positive Mental Attitude
Ingrisano, John R.
　　　　A Perfect Day: Reflections on Faith & Forgiveness
Jones, Francis A.
　　　　The Life Story of Thomas A. Edison
Kohe, Martin J.
　　　　Your Greatest Power
Mandino, Og
　　　　The Greatest Miracle in the World
　　　　The Greatest Salesman in the World
Manning, Brennan
　　　　The Ragamuffin Gospel
Maxwell, John C.
　　　　The Difference Maker
Osborn, Alex F.
　　　　Applied Imagination
　　　　Your Creative Power,
Packard, Vance
　　　　The Hidden Persuaders
Pausch, Randy
　　　　The Last Lecture
Peale, Norman
　　　　The Power of Positive Thinking

Peck, M. Scott
>The Road Less Traveled

Scott, Dru
>*How to Put More Time in Your Life*

Still, Henry
>*Of Time, Tides and Inner Clocks*

Stone, W. Clement
>*The Success System That Never Fails*

Walker, Harold
>*Power to Manage Yourself*

Warren, Rick
>*The Purpose Driven* Life

Webber, Ross A.
>*Time and Management.*

Winkler, John K.
>*John D., A Portrait in Oils*